国家出版基金项目
NATIONAL PUBLICATION FOUNDATION

国际海事组织海员行为示范

MODEL
COURSE 1.23

精通救生艇筏和除快速救助艇以外的救助艇

PROFICIENCY IN SURVIVAL CRAFT AND RESCUE BOATS OTHER THAN FAST RESCUE BOATS (2000)

中华人民共和国海事局 译

大连海事大学出版社
DALIAN MARITIME UNIVERSITY PRESS

国际海事组织 2000 年第一次出版

4 Albert Embankment, London SE1 7SR

图书在版编目(CIP)数据

精通救生艇筏和除快速救助艇以外的救助艇 = PROFICIENCY IN SURVIVAL CRAFT AND RESCUE BOATS OTHER THAN FAST RESCUE BOATS : 汉英对照 / 国际海事组织著 ; 中华人民共和国海事局译. — 大连 : 大连海事大学出版社, 2015.7

(国际海事组织海员行为示范)

ISBN 978-7-5632-3184-3

Ⅰ. ①精… Ⅱ. ①国… ②中… Ⅲ. ①船舶救生设备—技术培训—教材—汉、英 Ⅳ. ①U667.6

中国版本图书馆 CIP 数据核字(2015)第 144743 号

大连海事大学出版社出版

地址:大连市凌海路 1 号　邮编:116026　电话:0411-84728394　传真:0411-84727996

http://www.dmupress.com E-mail:cbs@dmupress.com

大连住友彩色印刷有限公司印装　　大连海事大学出版社发行

2015 年 7 月第 1 版　　2015 年 7 月第 1 次印刷

幅面尺寸:210 mm×297 mm　　印数:1~3000 册

印张: 9.5　　字数: 288 千

出 版 人:徐华东　　策　　划:徐华东

责任编辑:董玉洁　　责任校对:任芳芳

封面设计:解瑶瑶　　版式设计:孟　冀　解瑶瑶

ISBN 978-7-5632-3184-3　　定价:29.00 元

国际海事组织海员行为示范
编审委员会

主　任： 郑和平

副主任： 林　浦　　葛同林

委　员： 刘正江　　杨万里　　张安富　　周明顺
朱可欣　　于洪江　　陆立明　　陈永忠
王玉洋　　王长青　　陈国忠　　唐春辉
韩杰祥　　毛洪鑫　　李蕙兰　　饶滚金
石万里　　王兴琦

《精通救生艇筏和除快速救助艇以外的救助艇》

翻　译： 卫桂荣

审　校： 成春祥　　孟祥武　　王成海

CONTENTS

目 录

页码

Foreword

Since its inception the International Maritime Organization (IMO) has recognized the importance of human resources to the development of the maritime industry and has given the highest priority to assisting developing countries in enhancing their maritime training capabilities through the provision or improvement of maritime training facilities at national and regional levels.

Following the adoption of the International Convention on Standards of Training, Certification and Watchkeeping for Seafarers, 1978 (STCW), as amended, IMO has developed model training courses to assist Member States in the effective implementation of the Convention and in achieving a uniform global transfer of information and guidance to enhance the skills and competence of training providers. Model courses significantly assist trainers and instructors to improve the standard and quality of their existing courses and enhance the implementation of the standards prescribed by the STCW Convention.

Furthermore, Member Governments have recognized that a comprehensive set of model courses in various fields of maritime training help to supplement the standard of instruction provided by maritime academies and allow seafarers, administrators and other technical specialists employed in maritime administrations, ports and shipping companies to improve their knowledge and enhance their skills and competence in related specialized fields.With the generous assistance of donors, IMO has developed a range of model courses in response to these generally identified needs. Model courses are updated through a regular revision process, taking into account any amendments to the requirements prescribed in IMO instruments, any technological developments in the field, and modern methodology in delivering training.

These model courses may be used by any training institution in developing training programmes to effectively implement related IMO instruments.

Koji Sekimizu

Secretary-General

前 言

国际海事组织(IMO)自成立伊始就认识到人力资源在海运业发展中的重要性,并最优先考虑通过在国家和地区层面上提供或改善培训设备来帮助发展中国家增强其海事培训能力。

在经修正的《1978 年海员培训、发证和值班标准国际公约》(STCW)通过之后,IMO 即编写了示范培训课程，以便在有效实施该公约方面以及在全球取得信息和指导的统一传播方面帮助各成员国,提升培训提供方的技能和能力。示范课程明显有助于培训师和教员改善现有课程的标准和质量,并提升了对 STCW 公约所规定标准的实施。

此外,成员国政府已经认识到,海事培训诸多领域中的一套综合性课程有助于对海事院校的授课标准加以补充,并允许海员、行政管理人员以及其他在海事行政机关、港口和航运公司工作的技术专家增长知识并提升其在相关专业领域中的技能和能力。在捐助者的慷慨帮助下,IMO 编写了一系列示范课程,以应对那些普遍被发现的需求。示范课程通过定期修订程序得以更新,同时兼顾对 IMO 文件中规定要求的任何修订、在该领域中的技术进步以及实施培训中的现代方法。

任何培训机构在制订培训计划时可以使用这些示范课程,以便有效实施 IMO 的相关文件。

关水康司

秘书长

1.23 MODEL COURSE

Introduction

■ Purpose of the model courses

The purpose of the IMO model courses is to assist maritime training institutes and their teaching staff in organizing and introducing new training courses, or in enhancing, updating or supplementing existing training material where the quality and effectiveness of the training courses may thereby be improved.

It is not the intention of the model course programme to present instructors with a rigid "teaching package" which they are expected to "follow blindly". Nor is it the intention to substitute audio-visual or "programmed" material for the instructor's presence. As in all training endeavours, the knowledge, skills and dedication of the instructor are the key components in the transfer of knowledge and skills to those being trained through IMO model course material.

Because educational systems and the cultural backgrounds of trainees in maritime subjects vary considerably from country to country, the model course material has been designed to identify the basic entry requirements and trainee target group for each course in universally applicable terms, and to specify clearly the technical content and levels of knowledge and skill necessary to meet the technical intent of IMO conventions and related recommendations.

■ Use of the model course

To use the model course the instructor should review the course plan and detailed syllabus, taking into account the information provided under the entry standards specified in the course framework. The actual level of knowledge and skills and prior technical education of the trainees should be kept in mind during this review, and any areas within the detailed syllabus which may cause difficulties because of differences between the actual trainee entry level and that assumed by the course designer should be identified. To compensate for such differences, the instructor is expected to delete from the course, or reduce the emphasis on, items dealing with knowledge or skills already attained by the trainees. He should also identify any academic knowledge, skills or technical training which they may not have acquired.

By analysing the detailed syllabus and the academic knowledge required to allow training in the technical area to proceed, the instructor can design an appropriate pre-entry course or, alternatively, insert the elements of academic knowledge required to support the technical training elements concerned at appropriate points within the technical course.

Adjustment of the course objectives, scope and content may also be necessary if in your maritime industry the trainees completing the course are to undertake duties which differ from the course objectives specified in the model course.

Within the course plans, the course designers have indicated their assessment of the time which should be allotted to each learning area. However, it must be appreciated that these allocations are arbitrary and assume that the trainees have fully met all entry requirements of the course. The instructor should therefore review these assessments and may need to reallocate the time required to achieve each specific learning objective.

介 绍

■ 示范课程的目的

IMO示范课程的目的是协助海事培训机构及其教学人员组织和引入新的培训课程，提高、更新或补充现有的培训材料，以此改进培训课程的质量和培训效果。

本示范课程计划的意图并不是向教员呈交一个他们期望“盲目遵循”的“教学包”，其意图也不是用视听或“编排的”材料来代替教员的存在。在所有的培训努力中，知识、技能和教员的奉献是向IMO示范课程材料的受训者传授知识和技能的关键构成要素。

由于不同国家接受航海类培训的学员所处的教育体系和文化背景各不相同，所以示范课程采用通用术语设计，可以适应各课程受训目标人群的基本要求，并明确提出了需要满足的IMO有关公约及相关决议案所必需的技术内容、知识和技能的水平。

■ 示范课程的使用

为使用示范课程，教员应当审视课程计划和教学大纲细则，考虑课程框架中规定的入学标准所提供的信息。在审视过程中，应当牢记学员知识和技能的实际水准以及从前的技术教育水平，并应当识别出在教学大纲细则范围内由于学员实际入门水准与课程设计者假定的水准之间的差异，可能引起困难的任何部分。为弥补这些差异，希望教员将涉及学员已经掌握的知识和技能的项目从课程中删去或不做重视。此外，教员应当识别出学员可能还没有掌握的任何学术知识、技能或技术训练。

通过分析教学大纲细则以及技术领域培训所需的学术知识，教员可以设计出适当的预科课程，或者在技术课程中的适当处加入技术课程需要的学术知识。

如果完成该课程的学员在其所处的航海事业中要从事有别于本示范课程规定的课程目标的职责，则可能有必要调整课程的目标、范围和内容。

在课程计划中，课程设计者已经表明了其估计的、应分配给每一个学习部分的时间。但是，必须清楚的是，这些分配是主观的，并假设了学员完全符合本课程的入门要求。因此，教员应当对这些估计进行重新审视而且可能需要重新分配时间以符合每一个特定培训目标的需要。

Lesson plans

Having adjusted the course content to suit the trainee intake and any revision of the course objectives, the instructor should draw up lesson plans based on the detailed syllabus. The detailed syllabus contains specific references to the textbooks or teaching material proposed to be used in the course. An example of a lesson plan is shown in the instructor manual on page 92. Where no adjustment has been found necessary in the learning objectives of the detailed syllabus, the lesson plans may simply consist of the detailed syllabus with keywords or other reminders added to assist the instructor in making his presentation of the material.

Presentation

The presentation of concepts and methodologies must be repeated in various ways until the instructor is satisfied, by testing and evaluating the trainee's performance and achievements, that the trainee has attained each specific learning objective or training outcome. The syllabus is laid out in learning-objective format and each objective specifies a *required performance* or, *what the trainee must be able to do* as the learning or training outcome. Taken as a whole, these objectives aim to meet the knowledge, understanding and proficiency specified in the appropriate tables of the STCW Code.

Implementation

For the course to run smoothly and to be effective, considerable attention must be paid to the availability and use of:

- properly qualified instructors
- support staff
- rooms and other spaces
- equipment
- textbooks, technical papers
- other reference material.

Thorough preparation is the key to successful implementation of the course. IMO has produced a booklet entitled "Guidance on the implementation of IMO model courses", which deals with this aspect in greater detail.

Training and the STCW 1995 Convention

The standards of competence that have to be met by seafarers are defined in Part A of the STCW Code in the Standards of Training, Certification and Watchkeeping for Seafarers Convention, as amended in 1995. This IMO model course has been revised and updated to cover the competences in STCW 1995. It sets out the education and training to achieve those standards detailed in Chapter VI, Table A-VI/2-1 of the STCW Code.

Part A provides the framework for the course with its aims and objectives and notes on the suggested teaching facilities and equipment. A list of useful teaching aids, IMO references and textbooks is also included.

■ 教案

在为适应招收的学员以及课程目标的修正而调整课程内容之后，教员应当基于大纲细则拟定教案。大纲细则中有教科书具体的参考书目以及计划用于课程的教学资料。教员手册第93页上标有教案的范例。教案可以包括添加了关键词或提示语的大纲细则,以帮助教员授课,在这种情况下就没有必要调整大纲细则的培训目标。

■ 学员展示

必须以不同的方式反复讲授概念和方法，直到通过试验和评估学员的表现和成绩使教员感到满意:学员已经达到了每一个具体的培训目标或培训效果。教学大纲以培训目标的格式排列编排,而且每个目标规定了技能要求,或者学员必须能做的事情作为学习或培训的效果。从整体上看,这些目标的目的在于满足STCW规则相应表格规定的知识、理解和熟练。

■ 实施

为使课程顺利进行和卓有成效,必须充分注意下列资源的获得和使用:

- 完全合格的教员
- 辅助人员
- 教室或其他场所
- 设备
- 教科书、技术论文
- 其他参考资料

充分的准备是成功实施本课程的关键。IMO已经制定了“IMO示范课程实施指南”,它更加详尽地涉及了这一方面并作为本课程的一个附件包含在本课程中。

■ 培训和STCW 1995公约

船员必须达到的适任标准在《海员培训、发证和值班标准国际公约》(经1995年修正)的STCW规则的A部分中进行了规定。本IMO示范课程已经过修正和更新,覆盖了STCW 1995中的适任能力。它列出了达到STCW规则第Ⅵ章表A-Ⅵ/2-1中规定的标准所需的教育和培训。

A部分提供了附有目的、目标的课程框架,和对推荐的教学设施和设备的注释。另外它还包含了有用的教具、IMO参考书目和教科书的列表。

Part B provides an outline of lectures, demonstrations and exercises for the course. A suggested timetable is included, but from the teaching and learning point of view, it is more important that the trainee achieves the minimum standard of competence defined in the STCW Code than that a strict timetable is followed. Depending on their experience and ability, some students will naturally take longer to become proficient in some topics than in others. Also included in this section are guidance notes and additional explanations.

A separate IMO model course addresses Assessment of Competence. This course explains the use of various methods for demonstrating competence and criteria for evaluating competence as tabulated in the STCW Code.

Part C gives the detailed teaching syllabus. This is based on the theoretical and practical knowledge specified in the STCW Code. It is written as a series of learning objectives; in other words, what the trainee is expected to be able to do as a result of the teaching and training. Each of the objectives is expanded to define a required performance of knowledge, understanding and proficiency. IMO references, textbook references and suggested teaching aids are included to assist the teacher in designing lessons.

The new training requirements for these competences are addressed in the appropriate parts of the detailed teaching syllabus.

The Convention defines the minimum standards to be maintained in Part A of the STCW Code. Mandatory provisions concerning training and assessment are given in Section A-I/6 of the STCW Code. These provisions cover: qualification of instructors; supervisors as assessors; in-service training; assessment of competence; and training and assessment within an institution. The corresponding Part B of the STCW Code contains non-mandatory guidance on training and assessment.

The criteria for evaluating competence in Table A-VI/2-1 of the STCW Code are to be used in the assessment of the competences listed in the table.

As previously mentioned, a separate model course addresses Assessment of Competence and use of the criteria for evaluating competence tabulated in the STCW Code.

■ Responsibilities of Administrations

Administrations should ensure training courses delilvered by colleges and academies are such as to ensure those completing training do meet the standards of competence.

■ Validation

The information contained in this document has been validated by the Sub-Committee on Standards of Training and Watchkeeping for use by technical advisors, consultants and experts for the training and certification of seafarers so that the minimum standards implemented may be as uniform as possible. Validation, in the context of this document, means that the Sub-Committee has found no grounds to object to its content. The Sub-Committee has not granted its approval to the documents, as it considers that this work must not be regarded as an official interpretation of the Convention.

In reaching a decision in this regard, the Sub-Committee was guided by the advice of a Validation Group comprised of representatives designated by ILO and IMO.

B部分提供了课程中讲课、演示和练习的概要。其中包含一个推荐的时间表，但从教和学的角度来看，学员达到STCW规则规定的最低标准的适任能力比严格遵守时间表更加重要。依据其经验和能力的不同，有些学生自然地要在其中一些主题上花费更长的时间才能变得熟练。另外，这部分中还含有指导性说明和附加解释。

一个独立的IMO示范课程专门处理适任能力的评估。该课程阐述了如何使用不同的方法演示STCW规则中列出的适任能力以及评价适任能力的标准。

C部分给出了基于STCW规则规定的理论和实践知识的教学大纲细则。它是按一系列的培训目标编写的，换言之，将期望学员所达到的能力作为教和学的效果。每一个目标被扩展开来去界定所要求的知识、理解和熟练。IMO参考书目、教科书的参考资料以及推荐的教具也包含在内，以便协助教师设计课堂教学。

针对这些适任能力的新的培训要求，教学大纲细则中的相应部分已经过处理。

该公约在STCW规则A部分中规定了要保持的最低标准。有关培训和评估的强制性规定在STCW规则第A- Ⅰ/6节中载明。这些规定包括：教员的资格；作为评估员的监督员；在职培训；适任能力评估；以及院校内的培训和评估。STCW规则中相应的B部分载有培训和评估的非强制性指南。

评估表中所列的适任性时应适用STCW规则表A-Ⅵ/2-1中的适任性评价标准。

如前所述，一个独立的示范课程专门处理适任能力的评估并使用其标准评价STCW规则中列出的适任能力。

■ 行政管理职责

行政管理机关应当保证，由院校开设的培训课程要能保证满足适任标准。

■ 有效性

本文件中载明的信息已被培训和值班标准分委员会确认为有效，可供技术顾问和专家用于船员的培训和发证，以便使所实施的最低标准可以尽可能地得到统一。在本文件中，有效性是指该分委员会还没有找到反对其内容的根据。该分委员会也没有将其权威授予本文件，因为该分委员会认为不应将本文件视为是对公约的官方解释。

在这方面达成共识时，由ILO和IMO指定的代表组成的有效性小组提出的建议对该分委员会给予了指导。

Part A: Course Framework

■ Aims

This model course aims to provide the training for candidates to launch and take charge of a survival craft or rescue boat in emergency situations, in accordance with Section A-VI/2 of the STCW Code.

■ Objective

This syllabus covers the requirements of the 1995 STCW Convention Chapter VI, Section A-VI/2, Table A-VI/2-1. On meeting the minimum standard of competence in survival craft and rescue boats other than fast rescue boats, a trainee will be competent to operate life-saving appliances and take charge of a survival craft or rescue boat during or after launch. They will also be able to operate a survival craft engine and manage survivors and survival craft after abandoning ship. Trainees will know the correct use of all locating devices, including communication and signalling apparatus and pyrotechnics, how to apply first aid to survivors and the actions to take to preserve the lives of those in their charge.

■ Entry standards

For admission to the course, seafarers must be certified by a doctor to be in good health. They must also have completed the four basic courses covering the familiarization and basic safety training and instruction in accordance with Regulation VI/1 of STCW 1995.

■ Course certificate

On successful completion of the course and demonstration of competence, a document may be issued certifying that the holder has met the standard of competence specified in Table A-VI/2-1 of STCW 1995.

A certificate may be issued only by centres approved by the Administration.

■ Course intake limitations

The maximum number of trainees attending each session will depend on the availability of instructors, equipment and facilities available for conducting the training. It should not exceed the number of persons which the survival craft to be used is permitted to carry, and should not, at any time, exceed that which will allow sufficient opportunity for each trainee to have adequate practical instruction in procedures for the proper use of systems and equipment.

■ Staff requirements

The instructor shall have appropriate training in instructional techniques and training methods (STCW Code Section A-I/6, paragraph 7).

A部分:课程框架

■ 目的

本示范培训课程的目的是按照STCW规则A-Ⅵ/2节,向考证学员提供在紧急情况下释放和操作救生艇筏和救助艇的培训。

■ 目标

本课程大纲覆盖STCW1995公约第Ⅵ章第A-Ⅵ/2节表A-Ⅵ/2-1的要求,满足救生艇筏和除快速救助艇以外的救助艇的最低适任标准,学员将胜任救生设备的操作和在释放中或释放之后操作救生艇筏和救助艇,同时还将胜任救生艇筏机器的操作和在弃船后对求生者和救生艇筏的管理。学员将掌握所有定位设备的正确使用方法,包括通信设备、信号设备及烟火信号,掌握对求生者进行急救和维持艇上人员生命的措施。

■ 入学标准

因本课程之需要,参加本课程培训的所有船员必须经体检且合格。他们还应根据STCW1995第Ⅵ/1章的规定完成熟悉和基本安全等四门基本课程的培训和指导。

■ 课程证书

经全部完成本课程并表明适任后,培训证明书将被签发以证明持证人满足STCW1995表A-Ⅵ/2-1载明的适任标准。

培训合格证书只能由经主管机关认可的培训机构签发。

■ 课程人数限制

培训开班的规模视教员的人数、培训设备和设施的数量而定,以不超过使用的救生艇筏允许的安全定员为限,并且在任何时候不得过多,以确保每个学员有充足的机会,在适当使用系统和设备的程序方面,获得充分的实践训练。

■ 教员要求

从事培训的教员应经过适当的有关教学技能和培训方法的培训(STCW规则第A-Ⅰ/6节第7段)。

■ Training facilities and equipment

Ordinary classroom facilities and an overhead projector are required for the lecturers. In addition, a demonstration table measuring 3 m by 1 m would be an advantage. When making use of audio-visual material such as videos or slides, make sure the appropriate equipment is available.

The practical lessons require access to a lake or the sea, preferably in harbour or estuarial waters. A swimming pool could be used for certain of the wet drills.

The following items of equipment are required:

1 glass-reinforced plastic lifeboat, approximately 8 metres in length, fitted with an inboard diesel engine, and a full set of oars(new or replacement boats should preferably be fire-protected lifeboats complying with Section 6.1 of the LSA Code) with a set of gravity davits to house the lifeboat, sited so as to allow launching into the water

1 portable hoist unit suitable for recovery of the lifeboat

1 glass-reinforced plastic rescue boat with outboard engine and a full set of oars with a set of launching davits to house the rescue boat, sited so as to allow launching into the water

1 portable hoist unit suitable for recovery of rescue boats

2 20-man inflatable liferafts in containers, one of which can be placed in a float-free stowage with hydrostatic release unit

1 davit-launched inflatable liferaft with launching davit

Sufficient lifejackets for all trainees, instructors, rescue boat and fast rescue boat crews, immersion suits, thermal protective aids, anti-exposure suits

3 portable 2-way radiotelephones approved for use in survival craft

1 demonstration set of survival craft pyrotechnics

1 emergency position-indicating radio beacon (EPIRB) operating on 406 MHz

1 search and rescue transponder (SART) operating on 9 GHz

1 helicopter rescue sling

1 complete set of lifeboat equipment

1 complete set of liferaft equipment

1 life-size dummy for resuscitation training

1 Neil–Robertson stretcher for use in exercises

Safety/first aid equipment comprising:

- MOB boat
- powerful searchlights
- retro-reflective tapes①
- first-aid kit
- stretcher
- resuscitation kit with oxygen/suction unit

The practical drills and evaluation could be carried out aboard a ship, making use of its equipment and facilities.

---

① Necessary if drills are performed at night.

■ 教学设施和设备

要配有通用教室设施和一台投影仪供理论教学使用,另外配备一个3 m×1 m的演示台以便利教学。若采用录像或幻灯片等视听资料教学,还应配备相应的设备。

实操训练课程要求在湖泊或海上进行,也可在港口或港湾水域。某些水上训练可在游泳池进行。

要求配备下列设备:

1 条玻璃钢救生艇,约8 m长,装有内置艇用柴油机和全套桨(新购或重新更换的救生艇应根据"救生设备规则"第6.1节的规定采用防火救生艇),并配有一套能存放救生艇的重力式吊艇架,存放位置应能将救生艇放入水中

1 套可用于收回救生艇的轻便式吊艇装置

1 条玻璃钢救助艇,配有外置艇机和全套桨,并有1套能存放救助艇的释放架,位置应能将救生艇放入水中

1 套可用于收回救助艇的轻便式吊艇装置

2 只存放在容器中的可容纳20人的气胀式救生筏,其中一个配有静水压力释放器,处于自浮释放状态

1 只配有释放架的吊放式气胀式救生筏,供所有学员、教员、救助艇和快速救助艇艇员使用的足够数量的救生衣、防水救生服、保温器具、防暴露服

3 只认可的可供救生艇筏使用的双向手提式对讲机

1 套救生艇烟火信号展示品

1 只406 MHz无线电应急示位标(EPIRB)

1 只9 GHz搜救雷达应答器(SART)

1 条直升机营救吊绳

1 整套救生艇属具

1 整套救生筏属具

1 只供人工呼吸培训用的真人大小的人体模具

1 套演习用尼尔-罗勃逊(Neil-Robertson)担架

安全和急救设备包括:

—MOB救助艇

—强光搜索照明灯

—反光带[①]

—急救包

—担架

—配有氧气和吸入装置的复苏急救用具

实操训练和评估可在船上进行并使用船上的设备和设施。

---

① 夜间训练时需要。

Teaching aids (A)

A1 Instructor Manual (Part D of the course)

A2 Specimen muster list

A3 Specimen training and survival manual and on-board maintenance manual

A4 Videos:
V1 SOLAS Chapter III Part 1 – Preparing for Abandonment (Code No. 297.1)
V2 SOLAS Chapter III Part 2 – Abandonment by Lifeboat (Code No. 297.2)
V3 SOLAS Chapter III Part 3 – Abandonment by Liferaft (Code No. 297.3)
V4 SOLAS Chapter III Part 4 – Techniques of Survival (Code No. 297.4)
V5 SOLAS Chapter III Part 5 – SOLAS Amendments (Code No. 463)
V6 Personal Survival Part 1 (Code No. 645)
V7 Personal Survival Part 2 (Code No. 646)
V8 Cold Water Casualty (Code No. 527)
V9 Man Overboard (Code No. 644)
V10 Lifeboat On-load Release Mechanism (Code No. 596)
V11 Viking Inflatable Liferaft (Code No. 404)
V12 Viking Davit Launchable Liferaft (Code No. 405)
V13 Viking Marine Escape Slide (Code No. 274)
V14 Viking Marine Evacuation System (Code No. 275)

Bibliography (B)

B1 C.H. Wright, *Proficiency in Survival Craft Certificates*(Glasgow: Brown, Son and Ferguson, 1988) (ISBN 0-85174-540-7) (OUT OF PRINT)
B2 D.J. House, *Marine Survival and Rescue Systems* (London: Witherby & Co., 1977) (ISBN 1-85609-127-9)

IMO references (R)

R1 The International Convention on Standards of Training, Certification and Watchkeeping for Seafarers, 1995(STCW 1995), 1998 edition (IMO Sales No. 938E)
R2 International Convention for the Safety of Life at Sea, 1974(SOLAS 1974), as amended (IMO Sales No. 110E)
R3 IMO Life-Saving Appliances Code (LSA Code) (IMO Sales No. 982E)
R4 Merchant Ship Search and Rescue Manual (MERSAR) (IMO Sales No. 963E)
R5 A Pocket Guide to Cold Water Survival (IMO Sales No. 946E)
R6 LSA symbols – Poster (IMO Sales No. 981E)
R7 Assembly resolution A.660(16) – Carriage of satellite emergency position-indicating radio beacons (EPIRBs)
R8 Assembly resolution A.657(16) – Instructions for action in survival craft

■ 教具(A)

A1 教员手册(本课程D部分)

A2 应变部署表范本

A3 训练、求生手册和船上维护保养手册范本

A4 视频录像资料:
V1 SOLAS第Ⅲ章第1部分—弃船准备(IMO代码:NO.297.1)
V2 SOLAS第Ⅲ章第2部分—乘救生艇弃船(IMO代码:NO.297.2)
V3 SOLAS第Ⅲ章第3部分—乘救生筏弃船(IMO代码:NO.297.3)
V4 SOLAS第Ⅲ章第4部分—求生技能(IMO代码:NO.297.4)
V5 SOLAS第Ⅲ章第5部分—SOLAS修订案 (IMO代码:NO.463)
V6 个人求生第一部分(IMO代码:NO.645)
V7 个人求生第二部分(IMO代码:NO.646)
V8 冷水中的人员伤亡(IMO代码:NO.527)
V9 人员落水(IMO代码:NO.644)
V10 救生艇载员释放装置(IMO代码:NO.596)
V11 维京气胀式救生筏(IMO代码:NO.404)
V12 维京吊放式救生筏(IMO代码:NO.405)
V13 维京海上逃生滑道(IMO代码:NO.274)
V14 维京海上撤离系统(IMO代码:NO.275)

■ 参考文献(B)

B1 精通救生艇筏证书,C.H. Wright 著 (Glasgow:Brown,Son and Ferguson出版社1988年出版)(ISBN 0-85174-540-7)(已不再印刷)
B2 海上求生和救援体系, D.J. House 著 (london:Witherby & Co. 出版社1977年出版)(ISBN 1-85609-127-9)

■ IMO参考书目(R)

R1 1995年海员培训、发证和值班标准国际公约(STCW1995)1998年版本(IMO销售号码:NO. 938E)
R2 经修订的1974年国际海上人命安全公约(SOLAS1974)(IMO销售号码:NO.110E)
R3 IMO 救生设备规则 (LSA Code)(IMO销售号码:NO.982E)
R4 商船搜救手册 (MERSAR)(IMO销售号码:NO.963E)
R5 冷水中求生指南袖珍本(IMO销售号码:NO.946E)
R6 IMO 字母符号—广告标语(IMO销售号码:NO.981E)
R7 A.660(16)决议—配置无线电应急示位标 (EPIRBs)
R8 A.657(16)决议—救生艇筏的行动指导

R9 Assembly resolution A.694(17) – General requirements for shipborne radio equipment forming part of Global Maritime Distress and Safety System (GMDSS) and for electronic navigation aid

R10 Assembly resolution A.762(18) – Performance standards for survival craft two-way VHF radiotelephone apparatus

R11 Assembly resolution A.763(18) – Performance standards for float-free satellite emergency position-indicating radio beacons (EPIRBs) operating on 406 MHz

R12 Assembly resolution A.802(19) – Performance standards for survival craft radar transponders for use in search and rescue operations

R13 Assembly resolution A.809(19) – Performance standards for survival craft two-way radiotelephone apparatus

R14 Assembly resolution A.810(19) – Performance standards for float-free satellite emergency position-indicating Radio Beacons(EPIRBs) operating on 406 MHz

R15 Assembly resolution A.812(19) – Performance standards for float-free satellite emergency position-indicating radio beacons(EPIRBs) operating through the geostationary Inmarsat satellite system on 1.6 GHz

■ Textbooks (T)

No specific textbook is recommended for trainee use.

■ *Safety routines*

Safety precautions during drills should be drawn up by the instructors, having regard to the nature of the drills and the facilities in use. Trainees should be fully aware of the safety precautions and be closely supervised at all times.

During abandon-ship drills and exercises in handling survival craft, a rescue boat must be in constant attendance. Night drills must not be performed unless all trainees and instructors have been provided with lifejackets having retro-reflective material complying with LSA Code, section 1.2.2.7 fitted in accordance with the recommendation in Assembly resolution A.658 (16). The practice area must be illuminated by searchlights.

R9　A.694(17)决议—全球海上遇险和安全系统船用无线电(GMDSS)和电助航设备的一般要求
R10　A.762(18)决议—救生艇筏双向VHF无线电对讲机的性能标准
R11　A.763(18)决议—406 MHz漂浮释放式卫星无线电应急示位标(EPIRBs)的性能标准
R12　A.802(19)决议—救生艇筏雷达应答器的性能标准
R13　A.809(19)决议—救生艇筏双向无线电话的性能标准
R14　A.810(19)决议—406 MHz漂浮释放式卫星无线电应急示位标(EPIRBs)的性能标准
R15　A.812(19)决议—1.6 GHz 极地卫星系统的漂浮释放式卫星无线电应急示位标(EPIRBs)的性能标准

■ 教科书(T)

没有特定的教科书推荐给学员使用。

■ 安全规定

教员应拟订演习中的安全注意事项,并顾及演习的性质和使用的设施。学员应完全清楚这些注意事项,并时刻处于严格的监督之下。

在弃船演习和快速救助艇操纵训练中,一艘准备就绪的救助艇必须时刻待命。不得进行夜间演习,除非所有学员和教员配备了带有反光材料的救生衣,该反光材料应符合IMO救生设备规则1.2.2.7节且其装配符合A.658(16)号大会决议的建议。实操区域必须有探照灯照明。

Part B: Course Outline and Timetable

■ Lectures

As far as possible, lectures should be presented within a familiar context and should make use of practical examples. They should be well illustrated with diagrams, photographs and charts where appropriate, and be related to matter learned during seagoing time.

An effective manner of presentation is to develop a technique of giving information and then reinforcing it. For example, first tell the trainees briefly what you are going to present to them; then cover the topic in detail; and, finally, summarize what you have told them. The use of an overhead projector and the distribution of copies of the transparencies as trainees' handouts contribute to the learning process.

■ Course Outline

The tables that follow list the competencies and areas of knowledge, understanding and proficiency, together with the estimated total hours required for lectures and practical exercises. Teaching staff should note that timings are suggestions only and should be adapted to suit individual groups of trainees depending on their experience, ability, equipment and staff available for training.

B 部分:课程概要和时间表

■ 教学

教学应尽可能在一种海上常见的情境中进行,并尽可能采用实际案例,应以适当的插图、图片、图表清楚地予以说明,并结合海上航行中遇到的实际情况。

形成一种先传授信息,然后再予以强化的技巧,这是一种有效的授课方法。例如,首先简要说明你所要讲授的内容,然后详细讲解,最后总结概括你传授的内容。使用投影仪和分发幻灯片的复印件作为讲义将有助于学习过程。

■ 课程概要

下表列明了知识、理解和熟练的适任能力和范围以及理论授课和实操训练的预计时间要求。教员应注意时间安排仅仅是推荐时间,教员应根据各班组学员的经验、能力,可用培训设备和师资等实际情况进行适当的调整。

Course Outline

Course Outline	Approximate Time (Hours)
Knowledge, understanding and proficiency	**Lectures, demonstrations and practical exercises**
1 ***Introduction and safety*** 1.1 Introduction 1.2 Safety guidance	0.5
2 ***General*** 2.1 Emergency situations 2.2 Training, drills and operational readiness 2.3 Actions to be taken when called to survival craft stations	1.5
3 ***Abandon ship*** 3.1 Actions to be taken when required to abandon ship 3.2 Actions to be taken when in the water	0.5
4 ***Survival craft and rescue boats*** 4.1 Lifeboats 4.2 Liferafts 4.3 Rescue boats	0.75
5 ***Launching arrangements*** 5.1 Boat davits 5.2 Liferaft davits 5.3 Rescue boat davits 5.4 Free-fall 5.5 Float-free arrangements 5.6 Marine evacuation systems	1.25
6 ***Evacuation and recovery of survival craft and rescue boats*** 6.1 Launching 6.2 Clearing the ship's side 6.3 Marshalling liferafts and rescuing survivors from the sea 6.4 Recovery of survival craft and rescue boats 6.5 Launching survival craft and rescue boats in rough sea 6.6 Recovery of rescue boats in rough sea	1.25
7 ***Actions to take when clear of the ship***	0.25
8 ***Lifeboat engine and accessories*** 8.1 Starting the engine 8.2 Cooling systems 8.3 Battery charging 8.4 Fire extinguisher 8.5 Water spray system 8.6 Self-contained air support system	1.5
9 ***Rescue boat outboard engine***	1.0

课程概要

课程概要	预计时间 (小时)
知识、理解和熟练	教学、演示和实操训练
1　介绍和安全须知 1.1 介绍 1.2 安全须知	0.5
2　一般介绍 2.1 紧急情况 2.2 训练、训练和操作准备 2.3 召集到救生艇站时的行动	1.5
3　弃船 3.1 弃船时应采取的行动 3.2 水中求生应采取的行动	0.5
4　救生艇筏和救助艇 4.1 救生艇 4.2 救生筏 4.3 救助艇	0.75
5　艇筏释放装置 5.1 救生艇架 5.2 救生筏架 5.3 救助艇架 5.4 自由降落式吊艇架 5.5 漂浮释放装置 5.6 海上撤离系统	1.25
6　撤离和回收救生艇筏、救助艇 6.1 放艇 6.2 驶离船舶 6.3 集结救生筏和水中营救幸存者 6.4 救生艇筏和救助艇的回收 6.5 恶劣海况下救生艇筏和救助艇的释放 6.6 恶劣海况下救助艇的回收	1.25
7　驶离船舶时应采取的行动	0.25
8　救生艇机和艇上附属器具 8.1 启动艇机 8.2 冷却系统 8.3 电池充电 8.4 灭火器 8.5 喷水系统 8.6 自给式空气供给系统	1.5
9　救助艇外置艇机	1.0

Course Outline（continued）	Approximate Time (Hours)
Knowledge, understanding and proficiency	**Lectures, demonstrations and practical exercises**
10 Handling survival craft and rescue boats in rough weather 10.1 Boats 10.2 Liferafts 10.3 Beaching	0.75
11 Actions to take when aboard a survival craft 11.1 Initial actions 11.2 Routines for survival 11.3 Use of equipment 11.4 Apportionment of food and water 11.5 Action to take to maximize detectability and location of survival craft	1.5
12 Methods of helicopter rescue 12.1 Communicating with the helicopter 12.2 Evacuation from ship and survival craft 12.3 Helicopter pick-up	1.25
13 Hypothermia	1.0
14 Radio equipment 14.1 Two-way VHF radiotelephone apparatus 14.2 Emergency position-indicating radio beacons (EPIRBs) 14.3 Search and rescue transponder beacons (SARTs) 14.4 Distress signals, signalling equipment and pyrotechnics	1.5
15 First aid 15.1 Resuscitation techniques 15.2 Use of first-aid kit	2.0
16 *Drills in launching and recovering boats*	3.0
17 *Drills in launching liferafts* 17.1 Davit-launched liferafts 17.2 Throw-overboard liferafts 17.3 Boarding a liferaft from the water 17.4 Righting an inverted liferaft	3.0
18 Drills in launching and recovering rescue boats	3.0
19 Practical exercises and evaluation	6.0
TOTAL	31.5

Note: Teaching staff should note that outlines are suggestions only as regards sequence and length of time allocated to each objective. These factors may be adapted by lecturers to suit individual groups of trainees depending on their experience, ability, equipment and staff available for training.

课程概要(续表)	预计时间 (小时)
知识、理解和熟练	教学、演示和实操训练
10　恶劣海况下救生艇筏和救助艇的操纵 10.1 救生艇 10.2 救生筏 10.3 抢滩	0.75
11　在救生艇筏上应采取的行动 11.1 初始行动 11.2 求生者的常规知识 11.3 艇筏设备的使用 11.4 食品和淡水的分配 11.5 为最大可能地使救生艇筏被发现和定位应采取的行动	1.5
12　直升机营救方法 12.1 与直升机的通信联系 12.2 从船上和救生艇筏撤离 12.3 直升机吊运	1.25
13　体温过低	1.0
14　无线电设备 14.1 双向 VHF 无线电话设备 14.2 应急无线电示位标 (EPIRBs) 14.3 搜救雷达应答器 (SARTs) 14.4 遇险信号、信号设备和烟火信号	1.5
15　急救 15.1 复苏术 15.2 急救包的使用	2.0
16　救生艇释放和回收训练	3.0
17　救生筏的释放训练 17.1 吊放式救生筏 17.2 投放式救生筏 17.3 水中登救生筏 17.4 扶正倾覆救生筏	3.0
18　救助艇的释放和回收训练	3.0
19　实操训练和评估	6.0
合计	31.5

备注:教员应注意课程概要只是对分配给每一学习目标的顺序和时间的建议。教员可根据学员的经验、能力,可用培训设备和师资对这些要素做出调整以适应各班组学员的实际情况。

Course Timetable – Example

Day	Period 1 ($1\frac{1}{2}$ hours)	Period 2 ($1\frac{1}{2}$ hours)	Period 3 ($1\frac{1}{2}$ hours)	Period 4 ($1\frac{1}{2}$ hours)
1	1 Introduction and safety 2 General	2 General(continued) 3 Abandon ship 4 Survival craft and rescue boats	4 Survival craft and rescue boats (continued) 5 Launching arrangements	6 Evacuation and recovery of survival craft and rescue boats 7 Actions to take when clear of the ship
2	8 Lifeboat engine and accessories	9 Rescue boat outboard engines 10 Handling survival craft and rescue boats in rough weather	10 Handling survival craft and rescue boats in rough weather (continued) 11 Actions to take when aboard a survival craft	11 Actions to take when aboard a survival craft (continued) 12 Methods of helicopter rescue
3	13 Hypothermia 14 Radio equipment	14 Radio equipment (continued) 15 First aid	15 First aid (continued)	16 Drills in launching and recovering boat
4	16 Drills in launching and recovering boats (continued)	17 Drills in launching liferafts	17 Drills in launching liferafts (continued)	18 Drills in launching and recovering rescue boats (3 hours)
5	19 Practical exercises and evaluation	19 Practical exercises and evaluation (continued)	19 Practical exercises and evaluation (continued)	19 Practical exercises and evaluation (continued)

Teaching staff should note that the hours for lectures and exercises are suggestions only as regards sequence and length of time allocated to each objective.These factors may be adapted by lecturers to suit individual groups of trainees depending on their experience, ability, equipment and staff available for teaching.

课程时间表——示例

天	时段 1 (1.5 小时)	时段 2 (1.5 小时)	时段 3 (1.5 小时)	时段 4 (1.5 小时)
1	1 介绍与安全须知 2 一般介绍	2 一般介绍(续) 3 弃船 4 救生艇筏和救助艇	4 救生艇筏和救助艇(续) 5 艇筏释放装置	6 撤离和回收救生艇筏、救助艇 7 驶离船舶时应采取的行动
2	8 救生艇机和艇上附属器具	9 救助艇外置艇机 10 恶劣海况下救生艇筏和救助艇的操纵	10 恶劣海况下救生艇筏和救助艇的操纵(续) 11 在救生艇筏上应采取的行动	11 在救生艇筏上应采取的行动(续) 12 直升机救援方法
3	13 体温过低的急救 14 无线电设备	14 无线电设备(续) 15 急救	15 急救(续)	16 救生艇释放和回收训练
4	16 救生艇释放和回收训练(续)	17 救生筏的释放训练	17 救生筏的释放训练(续)	18 救助艇的释放和回收训练(3 小时)
5	19 实操训练和评估	19 实操训练和评估(续)	19 实操训练和评估(续)	19 实操训练和评估(续)

教员应注意讲课和训练的时间只是对分配给每一学习目标的顺序和时间的建议。教员可根据学员的经验、能力,可用培训设备和师资对这些要素做出调整以适应各班组学员的实际情况。

Part C: Detailed Teaching Syllabus

■ Introduction

The detailed teaching syllabus has been written in learning objective format in which the objective describes what the trainee must do to demonstrate that knowledge has been transferred.

All objectives are understood to be prefixed by the words, "The expected learning outcome is that the trainee................."

In order to assist the instructor, references are shown against the learning objectives to indicate IMO references and publications, textbooks, additional technical material and teaching aids, which the instructor may wish to use when preparing course material. The material listed in the course framework has been used to structure the detailed teaching syllabus; in particular,

Teaching aids(indicated by A),
Bibliography(indicated by B),
IMO references(indicated by R),
Textbooks(indicated by T) and
Audiovisuals(indicated by V)

will provide valuable information to instructors. The abbreviations used are:

Ch. chapter
col. column
pa. paragraph
Pt. part
Reg. regulation
Sect. section.

The following are examples of the use of references:

"R1–Sect. B-VI/2" refers to Section B-VI/2 of the STCW Code.

"R2–Reg. III/19.4" refers to regulation III/19, paragraph 4, of the 1974 SOLAS Convention.

■ Note

Throughout the course, safe working practices are to be clearly defined and emphasized with reference to current international requirements and regulations.

It is expected that the national institution implementing the course will insert references to national requirements and regulations as necessary.

C部分:教学大纲细则

■ 介绍

教学大纲细则按照学习目标的格式编写,在此格式中学习目标描述了学员必须要做的内容,以表明所传授的知识其已经掌握。

所有学习目标都冠以“预期的学习效果是学员……”的前缀,一目了然。

为了方便教员,针对学习目标列出了参考文献,并标明IMO参考书目和出版物、教科书、其他技术资料和教具,教员可以在准备教学资料时选用。在课程方案中列出的资料已作为教学大纲细则的组成部分;特别是:

教具(用A表示),
参考文献(用B表示),
IMO参考书目(用R表示),
教科书(用T表示)以及
视听教材(用V表示)

为教员提供了有价值的参考信息。使用下列缩写:

Ch. Chapter(章)
Col. column(栏)
Pa. paragraph(款,段落)
Pt. Part(部分)
Reg. regulation(规则)
Sect. section(节)。

以下是参考资料使用示例:

R1-Sect.B-Ⅵ2指STCW规则第B-Ⅵ/2节。

R2-Reg.Ⅲ/19.4指1974年SOLAS公约附则第Ⅲ条第19款第4段。

■ 注意事项

在授课过程中,要根据现行国际规则和规定对安全工作做法做出明确界定和强调。

期望实施课程的国内机构按照需要加入对国内要求和规则的引用。

Proficiency in survival craft and rescue boats other than fast rescue boats	IMO reference	Textbooks, bibliography	Detailed teaching syllabus reference
Competence: Take charge of a survival craft or rescue boat during and after launch **Knowledge, understanding and proficiency** *Construction and outfit of survival craft and rescue boats and individual items of their equipment.* *Particular characteristics and facilities of survival craft and rescue boats.* *Various types of device used for launching survival craft and rescue boats.* *Methods of launching survival craft into a rough sea.* *Methods of recovering survival craft.* *Actions to be taken after leaving the ship.* *Methods of launching and recovering rescue boats in a rough sea.* **Objectives are:**	R1–Sect. A-Ⅵ/2 Table A-Ⅵ/2-1		
1 right an inverted liferaft while wearing a lifejacket			17.4
2 interpret the markings on survival craft as to the number of persons they are intended to carry			4.1–4.3
3 give correct commands for launching and boarding survival craft, clearing the ship and handling and disembarking persons from survival craft			3.1,16.17,18
4 prepare and safely launch survival craft and clear the ship's side quickly			2.3,5,6,16,17,18
5 safely recover survival craft and rescue boats			6,16,18
Competence: Operate a survival craft engine **Knowledge, understanding and proficiency** *Methods of starting and operating a survival craft engine and its accessories together with the use of the fire extinguisher provided.* **Objectives are:**	R1–sect. A-Ⅵ/2 Table A-Ⅵ/2-1		
start and operate an inboard engine fitted in an open or enclosed lifeboat			8,9

精通救生艇筏和除快速救助艇以外的救助艇	IMO 参考书目	教科书、参考文献	教学大纲细则参考章节
适任:负责释放过程中和释放后的救生艇筏或救助艇 **知识、理解和熟练** 救生艇筏和救助艇的结构、属具及其各项设备; 救生艇筏和救助艇的特性和设施; 救生艇筏和救助艇的各种释放装置; 恶劣海况下释放救生艇筏的方法; 回收救生艇筏的方法; 离船后采取的行动; 在恶劣海况下释放和回收救助艇的方法。	R1—Sect. A-Ⅵ/2 Table A-Ⅵ/2-1		
培训目标:			
1 穿着救生衣扶正倾覆的救生筏			17.4
2 解释救生艇筏上用于表明乘载人员数目的标志			4.1-4.3
3 正确指挥救生艇筏的释放和登乘、驶离船舶、操纵艇筏及人员撤离艇筏			3.1,16.17,18
4 救生艇筏的释放准备和安全下水,迅速驶离船舶			2.3,5,6,16,17,18
5 安全回收救生艇筏和救助艇			6,16,18
适任:操作救生艇筏的机器 **知识、理解和熟练** 启动和操作救生艇筏机器及艇上附属设备; 使用所备灭火器的方法	R1—sect. A-Ⅵ/2 Table A-Ⅵ2-1		
培训目标:			
启动和操作开敞式或封闭式救生艇的内置机器			8,9

Proficiency in survival craft and rescue boats other than fast rescue boats	IMO reference	Textbooks, bibliography	Detailed teaching syllabus reference
Competence: Manage survivors and survival craft after abandoning ship **Knowledge, understanding and proficiency** *Handling survival craft in rough weather.* *Use of painter, sea-anchor and all other equipment.* *Apportionment of food and water in survival craft.* *Action taken to maximize detectability and location of survival craft.* *Method of helicopter rescue.* *Effects of hypothermia and its prevention, use of protective covers and garments, including immersion suits and thermal protective aids.* *Use of rescue boats and motor lifeboats for marshalling liferafts and rescue of survivors and persons in the sea.* *Beaching survival craft.* **Objectives are:**	R1–Sect. A-Ⅵ/2 Table A-Ⅵ/2-1		
1 row and steer a boat			7,10,16, 18
2 steer by compass			11.3,16,18
3 use individual items of equipment of survival craft			11
4 rig devices to aid location			14.2,14.3
Competence: Use locating devices, including communication and signalling apparatus and pyrotechnics **Knowledge, understanding and proficiency** *Radio life-saving appliances carried in survival craft, including satellite EPIRBs and SARTs.* *Pyrotechnic distress signals.* **Objectives are:**	R1–Sect. A-VI/2 Table A-VI/2-1		
1 use portable radio equipment for survival craft			14.1–14.3,
2 use signalling equipment, including pyrotechnics			14.4

精通救生艇筏和除快速救助艇以外的救助艇	IMO 参考书目	教科书、参考文献	教学大纲细则参考章节
适任:弃船后对求生者和救生艇筏的管理	R1—Sect. A-Ⅵ/2 Table A-Ⅵ/2-1		
知识、理解和熟练 在恶劣天气下操纵救生艇筏; 使用艇首缆、海锚及所有其他设备; 救生艇筏上食品和淡水的分配; 为最大可能地使救生艇筏被发现和定位应采取的行动; 直升机救援的方法; 低温效应及其预防,包括防水救生服、保温器具在内的保护遮盖物和衣服的使用; 使用救助艇、机动救生艇集结救生筏和营救入水者、求生者; 救生艇筏抢滩。			
培训目标:			
1　划桨和驾艇			7,10,16,18
2　利用罗经驾艇			11.3,16,18
3　使用救生艇筏各项设备			11
4　安设装置以帮助定位			14.2,14.3
适任:使用定位设备,包括通信设备、信号设备和烟火信号	R1—sect. A-Ⅵ/2 Table A-Ⅵ2-1		
知识、理解和熟练 救生艇筏上的无线电救生设备,包括卫星应急示位标(EPIRBs)和搜救雷达应答器(SARTs); 烟火遇险信号。			
培训目标:			
1　使用救生艇筏上的手提式无线电设备			14.1—14.3,
2　使用包括烟火信号在内的信号设备			14.4

Proficiency in survival craft and rescue boats other than fast rescue boats	IMO reference	Textbooks, bibliography	Detailed teaching syllabus reference
Competence: Apply first aid to survivors **Knowledge, understanding and proficiency** *Use of the first-aid kit and resuscitation techniques.* *Management of injured persons, including control of bleeding and shock.* **Objectives are:**	R1–Sect. A-Ⅵ/2 Table A-Ⅵ/2-1		
deal with injured persons both during and after abandonment, using first-aid kit and resuscitation techniques.			13,15

精通救生艇筏和除快速救助艇以外的救助艇	IMO 参考书目	教科书、参考文献	教学大纲细则参考章节
适任:对求生者进行急救 **知识、理解和熟练** 使用急救包和人工复苏的技能 伤员的处理,包括出血和休克的控制	R1—Sect. A-Ⅵ/2 Table A-Ⅵ/2-1		
培训目标:			
在弃船时和弃船后,使用急救包及复苏技能抢救伤员			13,15

Knowledge, understanding and proficiency	IMO reference	Textbooks, bibliography	Teaching aid
1 Introduction and safety (0.5 hour)	R1–Sect. B-Ⅵ/2		
Required performance:			A1
1.1 Introduction			
Required performance:			
1.2 Safety guidance			
.1 states the safety rules laid down			
.2 explains the use of the orders “STILL” and “CARRY ON” and the actions to take on hearing them			
2 General (1.5 hours)			A1
Required performance:			
2.1 Emergency situations			
Types of emergency			
.1 lists emergencies which may lead to abandoning ship as: – fire – collision – stranding – explosion – adverse reaction of dangerous goods or hazardous bulk cargo – shifting of cargo – foundering			
.2 lists the particular difficulties with regard to abandonment which may be encountered in the different emergencies			
.3 states that in the case of fire it may be prudent to launch some or all survival craft immediately to stand by while fire fighting continues			
.4 lists the emergencies that may require launching and operation of rescue boats as: – abandon ship, including marshalling of survival craft – man overboard – towing and rescue of survival craft from a shipwreck			
Emergency signals and public address system	R3–Sect.7.2		
.5 describes the general emergency alarm signal			
.6 lists the fire alarm signal and other alarms that may exist, e.g. smoke detector alarm			
.7 states that broadcast of emergency messages may also be made on public address system fitted in passenger and crew spaces and to muster stations			

知识、理解和熟练	IMO 参考书目	教科书、 参考文献	教具
1　介绍和安全须知(0.5 小时)	R1–Sect. B-Ⅵ/2		
技能要求:			A1
1.1　介绍			
技能要求:			
1.2　安全须知			
.1 说明已制定的安全规则			
.2 解释“停止”、“继续”指令的使用和听到该指令时应采取的行动			
2　一般要求(1.5 小时)			A1
技能要求:			
2.1　紧急情况			
紧急情况的种类			
.1 列举可能导致弃船的紧急情况: —火灾 —碰撞 —搁浅 —爆炸 —危险货物或有害散装货物的有害反应 —货物移动 —沉没			
.2 列举在不同的紧急情况下弃船可能遭遇的特殊困境			
.3 说明在发生火灾的情况下,作为安全措施,在灭火期间应立即释放部分或全部救生艇作为应急准备			
.4 列举可能需要释放和操作救助艇的紧急情况: —弃船,包括集结救生艇筏 —人员落水 —拖带和营救遇难船舶上的救生艇筏			
紧急信号和公共广播系统	R3– Sect.7.2		
.5 描述通用紧急报警信号			
.6 列举火灾报警信号和其他可能出现的报警,例如烟雾探测器报警			
.7 说明紧急信息还可通过安装在旅客舱室和船员舱室的公共广播系统播发,播送至应变集合地点			

Knowledge, understanding and proficiency	IMO reference	Textbooks, bibliography	Teaching aid
.8 states who would give the signal to abandon ship and how the signal might be made			
Muster list	R2–Reg. Ⅲ/37		
.9 lists the contents of a muster list			A2
.10 lists the duties assigned to members of the crew in relation to passengers			
.11 states that the person in charge of a survival craft, rescue boat or marine evacuation system must have a list of its crew			
.12 states that it is that person's duty to see that the crew are acquainted with their duties			
.13 states that the second in command should also have a list of the crew			
.14 states that the muster list specifies substitutes for key persons who may become disabled			
.15 states that the muster list specifies which officers are assigned to ensure that life-saving and fire appliances are maintained in good condition and are ready for immediate use			
.16 recognizes the symbols relating to life-saving appliances and arrangements	R6		
Required performance:			
2.2 Training, drills and operational readiness	R2–		
.1 explains the requirements for regular training and drills	Reg. Ⅲ 19.1,		A1
.2 states the requirements for abandon ship drills	19.3.1 19.3.2		V6
.3 states the requirements for on-board training and instruction in the use of the ship's life-saving appliances	Reg. Ⅲ/19.4		
.4 states that there is need to be familiar with all of the ship's life-saving appliances	Reg. Ⅲ/19.2		
.5 states the provision and contents of a training manual and on-board training aids	Reg. Ⅲ/35		
.6 states the requirement for operational readiness, maintenance and inspection	Reg. Ⅲ/20		A3
Required performance:			
2.3 Actions to be taken when called to survival craft stations			
.1 lists the personal life-saving appliances as: – lifejackets – lifebuoys – immersion suits – thermal protective aids – anti-exposure suits	R2–Reg. Ⅲ/19.3.3		V1,V5

知识、理解和熟练	IMO 参考书目	教科书、 参考文献	教具
.8 说明弃船信号应由谁发出和如何发出弃船信号			
应变部署表	R2– Reg.III/37		
.9 列出应变部署表的内容			A2
.10 列出船员在旅客安全方面的职责			
.11 说明负责救生艇筏、救助艇或海上撤离的人员必须有一份艇员名单			
.12 说明主管人员有职责检查船员是否了解自己的个人职责			
.13 说明副指挥也必须有一份艇员名单			
.14 说明应变部署表应列明关键人员在不能履行职责时的指定替代人员			
.15 说明应变部署表应列明指定负有确保救生设备和灭火设备并使之保持良好、随时可用状态职责的驾驶员			
.16 认识与救生设备及其布置有关的符号	R6		
技能要求:			
2.2 培训、演练和操作准备	R2– Reg.III 19.1, 19.3.1 19.3.2		A1 V6
.1 解释定期培训和演练的要求			
.2 说明弃船演练的要求	Reg. III/19.4		
.3 说明在船培训的要求和救生设备的使用须知			
.4 说明熟悉船上所有救生设备的必要性	Reg. III/19.2		
.5 说明培训手册和在船培训辅助资料的规定和内容	Reg. III/35		A3
.6 说明操作准备、维护和检查的要求	Reg. III/20		
技能要求:			
2.3 被召集到救生艇筏位置时应采取的行动			
.1 列出个人救生设备: —救生衣 —救生圈 —防水救生服 —保温器具 —防暴露服	R2–Reg. III/19.3.3		V1,V5

Knowledge, understanding and proficiency	IMO reference	Textbooks, bibliography	Teaching aid
.2 describes personal preparation for abandoning ship			
.3 states that the person in command of each survival craft should check that all crew are present and that crew and passengers are suitably dressed and have correctly donned lifejackets			
.4 describes the preparations which should be made for launching survival craft and deploying marine evacuation systems			
.5 explains that boats should only be lowered to embarkation deck level on instructions from the master			
.6 explains that marine evacuation systems should only be deployed on instructions from the master			
.7 states that persons assigned in the muster list should take two-way VHF radiotelephone apparatus, EPIRBs, SARTs and other items to their stations			A2
3 Abandon ship (0.5 hour)			
Required performance:			
3.1 Actions to be taken when required to abandon ship			
.1 states that a ship should only be abandoned on the orders of the master or person in charge of the ship	R1–Table A-VI/2-1 col.3		
.2 lists additional items which may be put into a lifeboat when time permits			
.3 describes the supervision of boarding lifeboats and rescue boats			
.4 describes the supervision of boarding liferafts through marine evacuation systems			
.5 describes the supervision of boarding davit-launched liferafts			
.6 describes how hand-launched liferafts should be boarded from the ship			
.7 explains the dangers of jumping on to inflatable liferafts			
.8 explains why every effort should be made to keep dry when boarding survival craft			
.9 states that the person in charge should ensure that all of the boat's crew are present and all occupants are seated, with safety belts fastened where appropriate, before lowering			
.10 states that a check should be made to ensure that hands and arms are clear of the boat's sides			

知识、理解和熟练	IMO 参考书目	教科书、参考文献	教具
.2 叙述弃船时个人的准备			
.3 叙述每一救生艇筏的指挥者应核对并确定所有人员已经到位,船员和旅客已适当地着衣和正确穿着救生衣			
.4 叙述应做好释放救生艇筏和布置海上撤离系统的准备工作			
.5 解释应按照船长的指令只将救生艇释放到登艇甲板的位置			
.6 解释应按照船长的指令布置海上撤离系统			A2
.7 说明根据应变部署表承担职责的有关人员应携带双向 VHF 无线电话设备,EPIRBs,SARTs 和其他设备到指定集合地点			
3 弃船(0.5 小时)			
技能要求:			
3.1 弃船时应采取的行动			
.1 说明只有在船长或船上负责人下达弃船命令时方可弃船	R1–Table A-VI/2-1 col.3		
.2 列出在时间允许的情况下可能带上救生艇的其他物品			
.3 叙述对登乘救生艇和救助艇的监督			
.4 叙述对通过海上撤离系统登乘救生筏的监督			
.5 叙述对登乘吊放式救生筏的监督			
.6 叙述如何在船上登上人工释放的救生筏			
.7 解释跳上气胀式救生筏的危险			
.8 解释为何登上救生艇筏时应尽最大努力使自身保持干燥			
.9 说明救生艇筏负责人应保证所有艇上乘员已经到达,在放艇前所有人员坐稳并系好安全带(如有)			
.10 说明应检查并保证所有人员的手、臂不伸到艇舷外			

Knowledge, understanding and proficiency	IMO reference	Textbooks, bibliography	Teaching aid
.11 states that inboard engines of lifeboat and rescue boats should be started			
.12 states that an outboard motor should never be started out of the water			
.13 states that a water spray and air support systems should be set to operate and the closure of hatches should be checked if launching into oil on the surface			
.14 states that a check should be made to see that it is clear below before lowering a boat, throwing a raft overboard, or deploying a marine evacuation system			
.15 explains what the person in charge should do if it proves impossible to launch a survival craft or deploy a marine evacuation system			
Required performance:			
3.2 Actions to be taken when in the water			V9
.1 states that a person should never enter the water without a lifejacket			
.2 states that an immersion suit, thermal protective aid or anti-exposure suit should be worn if available			
.3 explains that anything buoyant will help a survivor in the water			
.4 explains that a person in the water will cool and suffer from exposure very quickly, even in temperate areas, unless wearing an immersion suit, thermal protective aid or anti-exposure suit			
.5 explains that survivors in the water should swim to survival craft, buoyant wreckage or one another if within range, but otherwise avoid unnecessary exertion			
.6 describes the lifejacket light and whistle as an aid to rescue			
.7 explains how to hold on to a boat or raft			
4 Survival craft and rescue boats (0.75 hour)			A1
Required performance:			
4.1 Lifeboats	R3–Sect.4.4.1		V2.V3
.1 describes the construction and outfit of the following lifeboats: – partially enclosed – totally enclosed – free-fall – with a self-contained air support system – fire-protected			

知识、理解和熟练	IMO 参考书目	教科书、参考文献	教具
.11 说明应启动救生艇和救助艇的内置艇机			
.12 说明外置艇机的发动机在进入水前不可启动			
.13 说明如释放到有油面的水中，水喷淋和空气供给系统应设为操作状态,并应检查舱门的关闭状态			
.14 说明在放下救生艇、投放救生筏或布置海上撤离系统前,应检查水面是否清爽			
.15 解释如果证实不能释放救生艇筏和部署海上逃生系统,救生艇筏负责人应采取的措施			
技能要求:			
3.2 在水中时应采取的行动			
.1 说明人在没有穿着救生衣时不得进入水中			
.2 说明应尽可能穿着防水救生服,带上保温器具或穿着防暴露服			V9
.3 解释任何漂浮物都将有助于在水中的求生者			
.4 解释即使在温暖的区域,人在水中也会迅速受冷和遭受暴露之苦,除非穿上防水救生服,带上保温器具或穿上防暴露服			
.5 解释求生者在水中除非游向可及范围内的救生艇筏,漂浮的失事船舶或其他人，否则应尽可能避免不必要的大强度运动			
.6 叙述利用救生衣灯和哨笛帮助营救			
.7 解释如何抓牢救生艇或救生筏			
			A1
4 救生艇筏和救助艇 (0.75 小时)			
技能要求:	R3–Sect.4.4.1		V2.V3
4.1 救生艇			
.1 叙述下列救生艇的结构和属具: —半封闭式救生艇 —全封闭式救生艇 —自由降落式救生艇 —配有自给式空气供应系统的救生艇 —防火救生艇			

Knowledge, understanding and proficiency	IMO reference	Textbooks, bibliography	Teaching aid
.2 describes the particular characteristics and facilities of each type of boat listed in objective 4.1.1			
.3 interprets the markings on a lifeboat as to the number of persons it is permitted to carry	R1–Table A-Ⅵ/2-1 col.3		
Required performance:			
4.2 Liferafts	R3–Sect. 4.1		V6,V11
.1 describes the construction and outfit of: – inflatable liferafts – rigid liferafts			
.2 describes the stowage of liferafts			
.3 interprets the markings on a liferaft as to the number of persons it is permitted to carry	R1–Table A-Ⅵ/2-1 col. 3		
.4 describes the particular characteristics and facilities of each type of liferaft			
Required performance:			
4.3 Rescue boats	R3–Sect. 5.1		
.1 describes the construction and outfit of the following rescue boats: – rigid boats – inflatable boats – combination of rigid and inflatable boats			
.2 outlines the requirements for the carriage of survival craft and rescue boats in: – passenger ships – cargo ships	R2– Reg. Ⅲ/21 Reg. Ⅲ/31		
.3 describes the particular characteristics and facilities of rescue boats			
.4 states that arrangements for towing are permanently fitted in rescue boats	R3–Sect. 5.1.1.9		
.5 interprets the markings on a rescue boat as to the number of persons it is permitted to carry	R1–Table A-Ⅵ/2-1 col.3		
.6 states that inflatable rescue boats shall be maintained at all times in a fully inflated condition	R3–Sect. 5.1.3.11		
5 Launching arrangements (1.25 hours)	R1–Table A-Ⅵ/2-1 R2– Reg. Ⅲ/12, 17,23,33 R3–Sect. 6.1		A1 V10,V12
Required performance:			
5.1 Boat davits			
.1 describes the arrangements for stowage, securing, gripes, tricing pendants and the methods of launching and recovering boats with: – gravity davits – luffing davits – single-arm davits			

知识、理解和熟练	IMO 参考书目	教科书、参考文献	教具
.2 叙述目标 4.1.1 中列明的每一类救生艇的特性和设备			
.3 识读救生艇上关于允许载荷及人员数量的标志	R1–Table A-Ⅵ/2-1 col.3		
技能要求:			
4.2 救生筏	R3–Sect 4.1		V6,V11
.1 叙述下列救生筏的结构和属具: —气胀式救生筏 —刚性救生筏			
.2 叙述救生筏的存放			
.3 识读救生筏上关于允许载荷及人员数量的标志	R1–Table A-Ⅵ/2-1 col.3		
.4 叙述各种类型救生筏的特性和设备			
技能要求:			
4.3 救助艇	R3–Sect.5.1		
.1 叙述下列救助艇的结构和属具: —刚性救助艇 —气胀式救助艇 —刚性气胀式救助艇			
.2 简述下列船舶救生艇筏和救助艇的配备要求: —客船 —货船	R2–Reg.Ⅲ/21 Reg.Ⅲ/31		
.3 叙述救助艇的特性和设备			
.4 说明救助艇上的永久性拖带装置	R3–Sect. 5.1.1.9		
.5 识读救助艇上关于允许载荷及人员数量的标志	R1–Table A-Ⅵ/2-1 col.3		
.6 说明气胀式救助艇应始终保持在完全的充气状态	R3–Sect. 5.1.3.11		
5 释放装置(1.25 小时)	R1–Table A-Ⅵ/2-1		A1 V10,V12
技能要求:	R2–Reg.Ⅲ/12, 17,23,33		
5.1 救生艇架	R3–Sect. 6.1		
.1 叙述救生艇架存放、系固、固定、吊索等各种装置及其使用艇架释放和回收救生艇的方法: —重力式吊艇架 —升降式吊艇架 —单臂吊艇架			

Knowledge, understanding and proficiency	IMO reference	Textbooks, bibliography	Teaching aid
.2 describes methods of disengaging lifting hooks			
.3 outlines on-board maintenance of davits, falls and disengaging gear			
Required performance:			
5.2 Liferaft davits	R3–Sect. 6.1.5		
.1 describes liferaft launching davits			
.2 explains the operation of the automatic release hook			
.3 describes how the hook is recovered ready for launching another liferaft			
Required performance:			
5.3 Rescue boats davits			
.1 describes the arrangements for stowage, securing, gripes, tracing pendants and the methods of launching and recovering of rescue boats with: – gravity davits – luffing davits – single-arm davits			
.2 describes the methods of disengaging lifting hooks			
.3 states that rescue boat's launching appliance shall be fitted with a powered winch motor capable of raising the rescue boat from the water with its full complement of persons and equipment			
.4 states that means of launching from a position within the rescue boat is provided			
.5 states that foul weather recovery strops shall be provided for safety if heavy fall blocks constitute a danger	R2–Reg. Ⅲ/17.5		
Required performance:			
5.4 Free-fall			
.1 describes the arrangements for free-fall launching over the stern	R3–Sect. 6.1.4		
.2 explains that a secondary means of launching and for recovery of the boats is provided	R3–Sect. 6.1.4.7, 6.1.4.8		
Required performance:			
5.5 Float-free arrangements	R3–Sect. 4.1.6		
.1 describes the working of a hydrostatic release unit for a liferaft securing strap			
.2 explains the sequence of events leading to the release of the fully inflated liferaft in the case of a ship sinking	R2–Reg. Ⅲ/13 R3–Sect. 6.1.3		

知识、理解和熟练	IMO 参考书目	教科书、参考文献	教具
.2 叙述吊钩的脱离方法			
.3 简述船上吊艇架、滑轮、脱钩装置的日常维护			
技能要求:			
5.2 救生筏架	R3–Sect. 6.1.5		
.1 叙述救生筏的释放筏架			
.2 解释自动释放脱钩的操作			
.3 叙述如何将脱钩复位以释放另一救生筏			
技能要求:			
5.3 救助艇架			
.1 叙述下列救生艇架的放置、系固、固定,吊索装置及其释放、回收救生艇的方法: —重力式吊艇架 —升降式吊艇架 —单臂吊艇架			
.2 叙述吊钩的脱钩方法			
.3 说明救助艇释放装置应装有能够将救助艇、全部人员和设备从水中吊起的电动机绞车			
.4 说明装有可从救助艇内进行释放救助艇的装置			
.5 说明应配有恶劣天气回收索,以便在重型滑车滑轮构成危险时保证安全	R2–Reg. III/17.5		
技能要求:			
5.4 自由降落式			
.1 叙述安装在船尾上方的自由降落式释放装置	R3–Sect. 6.1.4		
.2 解释应提供释放和回收艇的备用方法	R3–Sect. 6.1.4.7, 6.1.4.8		
技能要求:			
5.5 漂浮释放装置			
.1 叙述救生筏系固索的静水力释放装置的工作机理	R3–Sect. 4.1.6		
.2 解释在船舶沉没时,导致完全气胀式救生筏释放的顺序	R2–Reg. III/13 R3–sect. 6.1.3		

Knowledge, understanding and proficiency	IMO reference	Textbooks, bibliography	Teaching aid
.3 describes the on-board maintenance of hydrostatic release units			
Required performance:			
5.6 Marine evacuation systems	R3–Sect 6.2		
.1 describes the construction and performance of marine evacuation systems			
.2 states the requirements of liferafts associated with marine evacuation systems			
.3 describes the containers for marine evacuation systems			
.4 interprets the markings on marine evacuation systems as to the capacity of the system			
6 Evacuation and recovery of survival craft and rescue boats (1.25 hours)			
Required performance:			
6.1 Launching	R3–Table A-Ⅵ/2-1		A1
.1 states the importance of seeing that it is clear below before lowering survival craft			
.2 explains how boat painters should be set up before launching			
.3 describes the use of bowsing-in tackles			
.4 explains how to bowse in the falls to reduce swinging while the boat is lowered			
.5 describes lowering the boat from the deck and from on board			
.6 describes the unhooking of falls or operation of disengaging gear			
.7 distinguishes between normal release and on-load release and states when each would be used			
.8 explains the difficulties which could arise if the ship is still making headway			
.9 describes the launching of davit-launched liferafts			
.10 explains that the bowsing lines and painter must be passed into the liferafts before lowering, to ensure that they do not snag on anything			
.11 describes the automatic release hook for davit-launched liferafts			
.12 states when to release the safety-catch on the hook			

知识、理解和熟练	IMO 参考书目	教科书、 参考文献	教具
.3 叙述船上静水力释放装置的日常维护			
技能要求:			
5.6 海上撤离系统	R3−Sect. 6.2		
.1 叙述海上撤离系统的结构和性能			
.2 说明海上撤离系统配套的救生筏的要求			
.3 叙述存放海上撤离系统的容器			
.4 识读海上撤离系统关于系统载荷的标志			
6 撤离和回收救生艇筏、救助艇(1.25 小时)			
技能要求:			
6.1 放艇	R1−Table A-Ⅵ/2-1		A1
.1 说明在放下救生艇筏前检查下方是否清爽的重要性			
.2 解释放艇前如何备好艇首缆			
.3 叙述系固滑车的使用			
.4 解释如何在放艇时使用系固滑车拉紧下降,以减少艇筏的摇摆			
.5 叙述从甲板和从船上降落救生艇			
.6 叙述救生艇滑车的脱钩或脱钩装置的操作			
.7 区分正常释放和载荷释放并说明各自使用的时机			
.8 解释船舶仍然保持前进时可能增加释放的难度			
.9 叙述吊放式救生筏的释放方法			
.10 解释在放下艇前必须将固定拉绳和首尾绳穿过救生筏,以保证不被任何东西缠绕			
.11 叙述吊放式救生筏的自动释放吊钩			
.12 说明打开吊钩保险栓的时机			

Knowledge, understanding and proficiency	IMO reference	Textbooks, bibliography	Teaching aid
Required performance:			
6.2 Clearing the ship's side	R1–Table A-Ⅵ/2-1		
.1 describes how to get clear of the ship's side in a lifeboat: – using the engine – under oars			
.2 describes how the painter can be used to assist in clearing the ship's side			
.3 describes how to clear the ship's side in a liferaft			
.4 explains the particular difficulty of getting away from the lee side of a ship			
Required performance:			
6.3 Marshalling liferafts and rescuing survivors from the sea	R1–Table A-Ⅵ/2-1		V9
.1 explains that rescue boats should be used to marshal liferafts clear and pick up survivors and persons in the sea	R2–Reg. Ⅲ/2.3		
.2 describes how to pick up a survivor from the water			
.3 describes how to bring an injured or exhausted survivor aboard a lifeboat			
.4 states that anyone entering the water to assist a survivor must have a line attached			
Required performance:			
6.4 Recovery of survival craft and rescue boats	R1–Table A-Ⅵ/2-1		
.1 explains the method of handling boats under power and oars while coming alongside a ship or quay			
.2 explains the use of the painter to aid keeping survival craft and rescue boats alongside			
.3 states that disembarkation from rescue boats should be in an orderly manner, giving priority to injured persons, ladies and children			
.4 states that the coxswain should be the last person to leave the survival craft or rescue boat and it would be his or her responsibility to check that the boat is secure			
.5 states that it would be prudent not to leave the boat unattended			

知识、理解和熟练	IMO参考书目	教科书、参考文献	教具
技能要求：			
6.2 驶离船舶	R1–Table A-Ⅵ/2-1		
.1 叙述在救生艇上使艇远离船舶的措施： —使用艇机 —利用划桨			
.2 叙述如何利用艇首索协助救生艇远离船侧			
.3 叙述如何在救生筏上使筏远离船舶			
.4 解释从船舶下风侧驶离的特殊困难			
技能要求：			
6.3 集结救生筏和从水中营救求生者：	R1–Table A-Ⅵ/2-1 R2–Reg. Ⅲ/1.3		V9
.1 解释应将救助艇用于集合救生筏和营救求生者及水中人员			
.2 叙述从水中营救求生者的方法			
.3 叙述如何把受伤或疲惫的求生者带上救生艇			
.4 说明入水协助求生者的救助人员须系上安全绳			
技能要求：			
6.4 救生艇筏和救助艇的回收	R1–Table A-Ⅵ/2-1		
.1 解释救生艇使用艇机和划桨靠泊船舶或码头的操纵方法			
.2 解释利用艇首缆来协助使救生艇筏和救助艇靠泊			
.3 说明应有序地离开救助艇，并优先让伤员、女士和儿童离艇			
.4 说明艇长应最后离开救生艇或救助艇并应负责检查艇筏的系固情况			
.5 说明不让艇筏无人值守是一种谨慎的做法			

Knowledge, understanding and proficiency	IMO reference	Textbooks, bibliography	Teaching aid
Required performance:			
6.5 Launching survival craft and rescue boats in rough sea	R1–Table A-VI/2-1		
.1 explains how to reduce the risk of danger to survival craft or rescue boats or of injury to occupants during lowering if the ship is rolling heavily			
.2 describes the use of oil to quell breaking seas along the ship's side			
.3 explains how to lower a boat into a heavy swell			
.4 describes how blocks may be lifted as soon as unhooked to prevent injury to occupants			
.5 explains the use of on-load release systems			
.6 describes method of getting clear from ship's side			
Required performance:			
6.6 Recovery of rescue boats in rough sea	R1–Table A-VI/2-1		
.1 describes arrangements for recovery strops			
.2 describes the method of recovery of rescue boats in rough sea			
7 Actions to take when clear of the ship (0.25 hour)	R1–Table A-VI/2-1		
Required performance:			
.1 states that boats and rafts should attempt to get about 1/4 mile clear of the ship			
.2 states that all attempts should be made to look for survivors in the water and take them on board			
.3 states that safety equipment such as SARTs and EPIRBs floating in the water shall be taken on board			
.4 states that communication with other survival craft should be maintained			
.5 states that all survival craft should attempt to come in the vicinity of each other			

知识、理解和熟练	IMO 参考书目	教科书、参考文献	教具
技能要求:			
6.5 在恶劣海况下释放救生艇筏和救助艇	R1–Table A-Ⅵ/2-1		
.1 解释在船舶严重横摇的情况下,降落艇筏时应如何降低危及救生艇筏或救助艇及伤害艇上人员的风险			
.2 叙述沿着船侧使用镇浪油			
.3 解释如何在狂涌中降落救生艇			
.4 叙述为避免伤害艇上人员,如何在脱钩的同时升高滑轮			
.5 解释载荷释放系统的使用			
.6 叙述驶离船舶的方法			
技能要求:			
6.6 恶劣海况下救助艇的回收	R1–Table A-Ⅵ/2-1		
.1 叙述布置回收用的滑车吊索			
.2 叙述恶劣海况下救助艇的回收方法			
7 驶离船舶时应采取的行动 (0.25 小时)	R1–Table A-Ⅵ/2-1		
技能要求:			
.1 说明救生艇筏应尝试驶离船舶约 1/4 海里			
.2 说明尽一切努力去寻找水中的求生者并将他们营救上艇			
.3 说明应当将诸如 SARTs、EPIRBs 等漂浮在水中的安全设备带到艇上			
.4 说明应保持与其他救生艇筏的通信联系			
.5 说明所有救生艇筏应努力尝试留在其他艇筏附近			

Knowledge, understanding and proficiency	IMO reference	Textbooks, bibliography	Teaching aid
8 Lifeboat engine and accessories (1.5 hours)	R1–Table A-Ⅵ/2-1		A1
Required performance:			
8.1 Starting the engine	R3–Sect. 4.4.6		
.1 checks levels of fuel and lubricating oil			
.2 checks that the gear lever is in neutral			
.3 follows manufacturer's instructions and sets controls			
.4 primes the fuel system, if necessary			
.5 starts engine and adjusts the throttle			
.6 checks oil pressure gauge and water cooling, if applicable			
.7 operates ahead and astern propulsion			
.8 stops engine and turns off fuel			
.9 explains how to clean the fuel tank and renew fuel filters			
.10 states the quantity of fuel required for a lifeboat			
Required performance:			
8.2 Cooling systems			
.1 describes the following cooling systems: – air-cooled – fresh-water-cooled – seawater-cooled			
.2 explains that fresh-water cooling systems require protection with antifreeze when trading to cold areas			
.3 states that the engine should be capable of running with the lifeboat out of the water for a minimum of 5 minutes			
Required performance:			
8.3 Battery charging			
.1 states that batteries for engine starting, searchlight and fixed radio installation can be charged from the engine			
.2 describes arrangements for charging batteries from the ship's power supplies			
Required performance:			
8.4 Fire extinguisher			
.1 describes how to extinguish a fuel fire with the extinguisher provided in the boat			

知识、理解和熟练	IMO 参考书目	教科书、参考文献	教具
8 救生艇机及附属器具(1.5 小时)	R1–Table A-Ⅵ/2-1		A1
技能要求:			
8.1 启动艇机	R3–Sect 4.4.6		
.1 检查艇机燃油和滑油的油量			
.2 检查变速杆已置于空挡位置			
.3 根据操作说明书设定控制值			
.4 必要时启动燃油系统			
.5 启动艇机并调节风门			
.6 如可行,检查油压计和水冷却系统			
.7 推进器正车和倒车操纵			
.8 停机并关闭燃油			
.9 解释如何清洁油箱并更换燃油滤器			
.10 说明救生艇要求的燃油数量			
技能要求:			
8.2 冷却系统			
.1 叙述下列各种冷却系统: —空气冷却系统 —淡水冷却系统 —海水冷却系统			
.2 解释当船舶航行在寒冷地区时,淡水冷却系统需要采取防冻措施			
.3 说明艇机应能在救生艇不在水中时运转最少 5 分钟			
技能要求:			
8.3 蓄电池充电			
.1 说明用于艇机启动、探照灯和固定式无线电设备的蓄电池可从艇机进行充电			
.2 叙述用船电对蓄电池进行充电的装置			
技能要求:			
8.4 灭火器			
.1 叙述如何使用艇上所备的灭火器扑灭油火			

Knowledge, understanding and proficiency	IMO reference	Textbooks, bibliography	Teaching aid
Required performance:			
8.5 Water spray system	R3–Sect. 4.9.2		
.1 states that fire-protected lifeboats are fitted with a water spray system which can be turned on or off			
.2 explains that the spray is driven by a self-priming pump that starts as soon as the boat enters the water			
.3 states that the system should be flushed with fresh water and completely drained after drills			
Required performance:			
8.6 Self-contained air support system	R3–Sect. 4.8		
.1 explains that all entrances and openings should be closed when using the self-contained air support system			
.2 states that the system will provide for the air to remain breathable and for the engine to run normally for not less than 10 minutes			
9 Rescue boat outboard engine (1 hour)	R3–Sect. 5.1.1.8		
Required performance:			
.1 describes the rescue boat's outboard engine, with special emphasis on: – securing arrangements, normal position during operation and tilted position when stowed – arrangements of fuel tank, connections and priming – cooling system – use of choke – starting, throttle and stopping the engine – changing the gear			
.2 lists the prestart checks			
.3 explains how to start a cold outboard motor engine			
.4 states that the manufacturer's specification for petrol/oil mixture should always be followed to avoid damage to the engine			
.5 lists the checks that are made when: – engine does not start – engine power is reduced – engine is running			
.6 states that starting of outboard motor out of water will quickly heat the engine and will result in seizing of the engines			
.7 explains that outboard engines should never be laid horizontally, when transporting or stowing, as cooling water may drain into the engine			
.8 demonstrates the emergency stop device and method of operation			

知识、理解和熟练	IMO 参考书目	教科书、参考文献	教具
技能要求:			
8.5 水喷淋系统	R3–Sect. 4.9.2		
.1 说明防火救生艇装有可开关的水喷淋系统			
.2 解释由自吸泵驱动的水喷淋系统在救生艇进入水中就立即启动			
.3 解释该系统在演习后应用淡水进行冲洗并彻底将水排干			
技能要求:			
8.6 自给式空气供给系统	R3–Sect. 4.8		
.1 解释在使用自给式空气供给系统时，应关闭所有入口和开口			
.2 说明系统所提供的空气，在保持人员的正常呼吸和机器的正常运转情况下不少于 10 分钟			
9 救助艇的外挂艇机（1 小时）	R3–Sect. 5.1.1.8		
技能要求:			
.1 叙述救助艇的外挂艇机,重点介绍下列部分: —在正常使用位置和翘起存放位置的系固装置 —油箱的布置、连接和注油 —冷却系统 —节气门的使用 —启动、油门调节和停机 —变挡			
.2 列出启动前的检查			
.3 解释如何启动冷的外挂艇机			
.4 说明应严格按照产品说明书的汽油/混合油类规格，避免损坏机器			
.5 列出在下列情况下对机器的检查: —机器没有启动 —机器马力下降 —机器运转时			
.6 说明在水面上启动外挂艇机将使机器快速发热并导致机器停止运转			
.7 解释在运输和存放等任何情况下,外挂艇机均不可水平放置,防止冷却水进入机器			
.8 演示应急停车装置及其操作方法			

Knowledge, understanding and proficiency	IMO reference	Textbooks, bibliography	Teaching aid
.9 describes the onboard maintenance of outboard motor engines			
.10 states that turning the boat at high speed may capsize the boat			
10 Handling survival craft and rescue boats in rough weather (0.75 hour)	R1–Table A-VI/2-1		A1
Required performance:			
10.1 Boats			
.1 describes the use of the sea-anchor and how to rig an oil bag			
.2 describes the use of the steering oar when lying to a sea-anchor			
.3 explains how to heave-to when running before the wind			
Required performance:			
10.2 Liferafts			
.1 explains that in strong winds great difficulty will be experienced in getting clear of the lee side of a ship			
.2 explains how to position survivors to minimize the danger of capsizing when lying to a sea-anchor			
.3 explains the precautions when lashing a liferaft to other survival craft in rough weather			
Required performance:			
10.3 Beaching	R1–Table A-VI/2-1		
.1 states the types of beaches to be avoided if possible			
.2 states that, when possible, beaching should be undertaken in daylight			
.3 describes how to beach a boat under oars through surf			
.4 describes how to beach a boat under power			
.5 explains that persons should leave a boat over the stern to avoid being swept back to sea by the undertow			
.6 explains that an effort should be made to save the boat and its gear			
.7 describes the landing signals for the guidance of small boats with crews or persons in distress			
.8 describes how to beach a liferaft			
.9 states that all gear should be secured and the entrances opened to allow rapid escape			

知识、理解和熟练	IMO 参考书目	教科书、参考文献	教具
.9 叙述外置艇机发动机的日常维护			
.10 说明救生艇在高速时转向可能导致倾覆			
10 恶劣海况下救生艇筏和救助艇的操纵 (0.75小时)	R1–Table A-Ⅵ/2-1		
技能要求:			A1
10.1 救生艇			
.1 叙述海锚的使用和如何放置镇浪油包			
.2 叙述在放置海锚时如何使用舵桨			
.3 解释如何在顺风行驶时顶风停船			
技能要求:			
10.2 救生筏			
.1 解释在强风中驶离船舶下风侧可能遇到的巨大困难			
.2 解释在放置海锚时如何安置筏上人员以将倾覆的危险降至最低			
.3 解释在恶劣天气下将救生筏绑扎到其他救生艇筏时的安全预防措施			
技能要求:			
10.3 抢滩	R1–Table A-Ⅵ/2-1		
.1 说明在可能时应避免抢滩的海滩类型			
.2 说明抢滩应尽可能在白天进行			
.3 叙述救生艇在划桨情况下利用海浪抢滩的方法			
.4 叙述救生艇使用动力抢滩的方法			
.5 解释抢滩后,人员应从船的尾部离开以避免被回头浪卷入海中			
.6 解释应尽力保全艇筏及其设备			
.7 叙述引导小艇及其船员或遇险人员的登陆信号			
.8 叙述救生筏如何抢滩			
.9 说明应系固所有的设备和打开入口以便迅速逃生			

Knowledge, understanding and proficiency	IMO reference	Textbooks, bibliography	Teaching aid
.10 explains that the raft should be carried clear of the beach to provide continuing shelter for survivors			
11 Actions to take when aboard a survival craft (1.5 hours)	R1–Table A-VI/2-1		A1
Required performance:			
11.1 Initial actions			
.1 states that survivors in water should be taken on board			V4
.2 explains the need to give first aid to injured, giving priority to resuscitation			
.3 states that all persons on board should be given anti-seasickness tablets			
.4 describes how survival craft should be secured together with the painter			
.5 explains the use of sea-anchors			
.6 lists immediate actions as: – streaming the sea-anchor – setting an EPIRB to function – erecting the canopy in boats – issuing anti-seasickness pills – bailing the craft dry – treating the injured – inflating the liferaft floor in cold conditions – getting radio equipment ready – posting lookouts			
.7 explains the need to ventilate a liferaft after it has been inflated before closing the openings			
.8 states that instructions on how to survive are contained in liferafts			
Required performance:			
11.2 Routines for survival	R8		
.1 explains that the person in charge should do everything possible to maintain morale			
.2 explains that organizing survivors to undertake tasks for their safety and comfort helps to maintain morale			
.3 states the importance of maintaining a constant lookout			
.4 lists the instructions which should be given to the lookouts			
.5 lists other tasks which should be assigned to crew members			
.6 states the main dangers to survivors			

知识、理解和熟练	IMO 参考书目	教科书、参考文献	教具
.10 解释救生筏应带离海滩,以便继续作为求生者的遮蔽物			
11 在救生艇筏上应采取的行动(1.5 小时)	R1–Table A-Ⅵ/2-1		A1
技能要求:			
11.1 初始行动			V4
.1 说明水中的求生者都应营救上艇			
.2 解释需对受伤者进行急救,并优先考虑进行复苏术			
.3 说明应向艇上的所有人员派发晕船药片			
.4 叙述如何将救生艇筏与首尾缆系牢			
.5 解释海锚的使用			
.6 列出应立即采取的行动: —投放海锚 —设置使用 EPIRB —支起艇上的帐篷 —发放晕船药片 —处理艇上的积水 —治疗受伤人员 —在寒冷条件下使救生筏的底部充气 —备妥无线电设备 —安排瞭望人员			
.7 解释气胀后的救生筏在关闭开口前需进行必要的通风			
.8 说明在救生筏中应备有求生须知			
技能要求:			
11.2 求生者的常规知识	R8		
.1 解释艇上负责人应尽一切可能保持人员的求生意志			
.2 解释组织求生者着手自身安全工作和安慰他们,以帮助保持求生信心			
.3 说明保持持续瞭望的重要性			
.4 列出瞭望人员的瞭望须知			
.5 列出船员被指派的其他工作			
.6 说明求生者的主要危险			

Knowledge, understanding and proficiency	IMO reference	Textbooks, bibliography	Teaching aid
Required performance:			
11.3 Use of equipment			
.1 lists the normal equipment of a lifeboat	R1–Table A-VI/2-1		
.2 lists the normal equipment of a rescue boat	R1–Sect. 4.4.8		
.3 lists the special equipment of an inflated rescue boat	R3–Sect. 5.1.2		
.4 lists the normal equipment of a liferaft	R3–Sect. 5.1.2.4		
.5 describes the use of each piece of equipment	R3–Sect. 4.1.5		
.6 describes the stowage of the equipment			
.7 explains that equipment not actually in use should be stowed in lockers or containers or lashed down so that it will not be lost in the event of a capsize			
.8 describes the markings on a boat compass card			
Required performance:			
11.4 Apportionment of food and water	R1–Table A-VI/2-1		
.1 states the quantities of food and water carried in a: – lifeboat	R3–Sect. 4.4.8.9, 4.4.8.12		
– liferaft	Sect. 4.1.5.18, 4.1.5.19		
.2 explains how to ration and issue water and emergency food			
.3 explains the dangers of drinking seawater			
.4 describes the arrangements for collecting rain water and how to store it			
.5 states that eating fish or foods other than the survival craft rations increases dehydration			
.6 explains how to minimize dehydration in hot conditions			
Required performance:			
11.5 Action to take to maximize detectability and location of survival craft			
.1 lists the equipment that may aid detectability and location of survival craft as: – EPIRB – SART – radar reflector – 2-way VHF radio			

知识、理解和熟练	IMO 参考书目	教科书、参考文献	教具
技能要求：			
11.3 设备的使用			
.1 列出救生艇的常用设备	R1–Table A-Ⅵ/2-1		
.2 列出救助艇的常用设备	R1–Sect. 4.4.8		
.3 列出气胀式救助艇的特殊设备	R3–Sect. 5.1.2		
.4 列出救生筏的常用设备	R3–Sect. 5.1.2.4		
.5 叙述每一件设备的使用方法	R3–Sect. 4.1.5		
.6 叙述各种设备的存放方法			
.7 解释设备在不用时，应存放在储物柜或容器内或绑紧固定,以便发生倾覆时不至于丢失			
.8 叙述救生艇罗经刻度盘的标志			
技能要求:			
11.4 食品和淡水的分配	R1–Table A-Ⅵ/2-1		
.1 说明下列救生设备携带的食品和淡水的数量： —救生艇 —救生筏	R3–Sect. 4.4.8.9, 4.4.8.12 Sect. 4.1.5.18, 4.1.5.19		
.2 叙述如何定量配给和发放淡水和应急食品			
.3 解释饮用海水的危害			
.4 叙述收集雨水的装置和如何存储			
.5 说明吃鱼或除救生艇筏的定量供给外的其他食品会增加脱水			
.6 解释在酷热条件下如何最大程度地减少脱水			
技能要求:			
11.5 为最大可能地使救生艇筏被发现和定位应采取的行动			
.1 列出救生艇筏上可协助被探测和定位的设备： —无线电应急示位标 (EPIRB) —雷达应答器(SART) —雷达反射器 —双向甚高频(VHF)无线电话			

Knowledge, understanding and proficiency	IMO reference	Textbooks, bibliography	Teaching aid
12 Methods of helicopter rescue (1.25 hours)	R1–Table A-VI/2-1		A1
Required performance:			
12.1 Communicating with the helicopter	R4		V7
.1 demonstrates the hand and arm hoisting signals			
.2 states that search and rescue service helicopters can communicate on VHF channel 16			
.3 explains that information may be passed to the helicopter through shore-based radio stations to Rescue Co-ordination Centre if suitable equipment is available			
.4 states that visual signals may be used			
.5 describes the information to shore radio station from survival craft that contains fullest possible detailed information for detection from air			
Required performance:			
12.2 Evacuation from ship and survival craft			
.1 describes the requirements for a helicopter pick-up area on board			
.2 explains the importance of lighting obstructions, such as masts and funnel, at night			
.3 describes the fire-fighting preparation for oil fire that should be kept ready			
.4 states that on no account should the helicopter winch cable be secured to any part of the ship			
.5 states that lifejackets should be worn during evacuation by helicopter			
.6 describes the means of evacuation from lifeboats and liferafts			
.7 describes precautions against being turned over in a liferaft by the helicopter's down-draught			
Required performance:			
12.3 Helicopter pick-up			
.1 describes methods of lifting persons by means of a: – rescue sling – rescue basket – rescue net – rescue litter – rescue seat			
.2 describes a rescue sling			
.3 explains that an injured person should be transferred from the ship's stretcher to the litter provided by the helicopter			

知识、理解和熟练	IMO 参考书目	教科书、参考文献	教具
12 直升机救援方法 (1.25 小时)	R1−Table A-Ⅵ/2-1		A1
技能要求:			
12.1 与直升机的通信联系			
.1 演示手臂升降信号	R4		V7
.2 说明可在 VHF 16 频道与搜救服务直升机联系			
.3 解释若有可用的适当的设备,信息可通过海岸电台转至搜救协调中心后再传送到直升机			
.4 说明可使用的其他视觉信号			
.5 叙述救生艇筏上传到海岸电台的信息,应含有最可能详尽的便于从空中探测的资料			
技能要求:			
12.2 从船舶和救生艇筏撤离			
.1 叙述船上直升机搭乘区的要求			
.2 解释夜间在船上诸如桅杆、烟囱之类的障碍物上照明的重要性			
.3 叙述应做好油类火灾的消防准备工作			
.4 说明决不能将直升机的升降索固定在船上的任何部位			
.5 说明从直升机撤离时应穿好救生衣			
.6 叙述从救生艇和救生筏撤离的方法			
.7 叙述因直升机的下降气流导致救生筏翻转的预防措施			
技能要求:			
12.3 直升机吊运			
.1 叙述用下列工具吊运人员的方法: —救生吊索 —救生篮 —救生网 —救生担架 —救生吊座			
.2 描述救生吊索			
.3 解释受伤人员应从船上担架转运到直升机专用营救担架上的措施			

Knowledge, understanding and proficiency	IMO reference	Textbooks, bibliography	Teaching aid
.4 describes how a member of the helicopter crew may as sist in picking up survivors			
.5 demonstrates the correct way to don a rescue sling and adopt a safe posture in it			
13 Hypothermia (1 hour)			
Required performance:	R1–Table A-Ⅵ/2-1		V8
.1 states the cause of hypothermia			
.2 describes the precautions to take to avoid hypothermia			
.3 describes the use of immersion suits, thermal protective aids and anti-exposure suits			
.4 describes the symptoms of hypothermia	R5		
.5 explains that heartbeat and breathing may be very feeble and difficult to detect in severe cases, but heart compression and artificial respiration will do more harm than good			
.6 describes how to treat a person suffering from hypothermia in a survival craft			
14 Radio equipment (1.5 hours)	R1–Table A-Ⅵ/2-1 R2–Reg Ⅲ/6.2 R4,R9, R10,R13		
Required performance:			
14.1 Two-way VHF radiotelephone apparatus			
.1 outlines the requirements of two-way VHF radiotelephone apparatus carried on passenger ships and cargo ships			
.2 states that the equipment is portable and capable of being used for on-scene communication between survival craft and rescue unit			
.3 states that a fixed two-way VHF radiotelephone may additionally be fitted on survival craft			
.4 states that the apparatus is capable of operation on frequency 156.8 MHz (VHF channel 16) and on at least one additional channel			
.5 demonstrates the controls and indicators of the equipment			
.6 states that the equipment is operational within 5 seconds of switching on			
.7 explains the transmitter power, receiver parameters, antenna type and receiver output			
.8 states that the power supply has sufficient capacity for 8 hours operation			

知识、理解和熟练	IMO 参考书目	教科书、 参考文献	教具
.4 描述直升机乘员如何协助吊运求生者			
.5 演示救生吊索的正确穿戴方法和采用安全的姿势			
13 体温过低(1 小时)	R1–Table A-Ⅵ/2-1		
技能要求:			
.1 说明体温过低的原因			V8
.2 叙述为避免体温过低应采取的预防措施			
.3 叙述防水救生服、保温器具和防暴露服的使用			
.4 描述体温过低的症状	R5		
.5 解释体温过低重症者的心跳和呼吸非常微弱，甚至难以探测,但心脏按压和人工呼吸将更为有害			
.6 叙述如何在救生艇筏上对体温过低人员进行急救			
14 无线电设备(1.5 小时)	R1–Table A-Ⅵ/2-1 R2–Reg. Ⅲ/6.2 R4,R9, R10,R13		
技能要求:			
14.1 双向 VHF 无线电话设备			
.1 简述客船和货船双向 VHF 无线电话的配备要求			
.2 说明该设备是手提式的,能够用于救生艇筏和救助艇之间的现场通信			
.3 说明在救生艇筏上可额外安装一套固定式双向 VHF 无线电话设备			
.4 说明该设备可在 156.8 MHz 频率(VHF CH16)和至少一个其他频道上工作			
.5 演示设备的控制器和显示器			
.6 说明该设备应在开机 5 秒钟内正常工作			
.7 解释设备的发射功率、接收参数、天线类型和接收机输出			
.8 说明设备的电源应有不少于 8 小时的工作容量			

Knowledge, understanding and proficiency	IMO reference	Textbooks, bibliography	Teaching aid
.9 describes the arrangement of the power supply and requirements with respect to primary batteries of portable two-way VHF radiotelephone apparatus			
Required performance:			
14.2 Emergency position-indicating radio beacons (EPIRBs)	R2–Reg. Ⅳ/7.1.6, 8.3		
.1 states the requirement for the carriage of EPIRBs in survival craft	R7		
.2 describes survival craft EPIRBs			
.3 states that they are capable only of manual activation and deactivation			
.4 states that the apparatus will operate for a period of 48 hours			
.5 states that survival craft EPIRBs operate on the aeronautical distress frequency	R11		
.6 describes a ship's satellite EPIRB operating on 406 MHz with 121.5 MHz beacon for homing by aircraft	R14		
.7 states that it is automatically activated after floating free			
.8 demonstrates the manual activation and deactivation of the EPIRB			
.9 states that the EPIRB will operate for a period of at least 48 hours			
.10 states that a satellite EPIRB transmits a distress message to a polar orbiting satellite for re-transmission to special receiving stations			
.11 describes a ship's satellite EPIRB operating on 1.6 GHz	R15		
.12 describes an EPIRB for sea area A1			
Required performance:			
14.3 Search and rescue transponder beacons (SARTs)	R2–Reg. Ⅲ/6.2.2		
.1 states the requirements of carriage of SARTs in survival craft	R12		
.2 describes the SART			
.3 states that a SART operates on 9 GHz			
.4 states that they are capable of manual activation and deactivation and that provision of automatic activation may be provided			
.5 states that the apparatus will operate in standby condition for 96 hours and in addition, following the standby position, will provide transmission for 8 hours when being continuously interrogated			

知识、理解和熟练	IMO 参考书目	教科书、参考文献	教具
.9 叙述设备的电源装置和关于手提式双向 VHF 无线电话设备原电池的要求			
技能要求:			
14.2 应急无线电示位标(EPIRBs)	R2–Reg. Ⅳ/7.1.6, 8.3 R7		
.1 说明救生艇筏应急无线电示位标的配备要求			
.2 叙述救生艇筏应急无线电示位标(EPIRBs)			
.3 说明 EPIRBs 只能人工启动和关闭			
.4 说明 EPIRBs 能工作 48 小时			
.5 说明 EPIRBs 工作在航空遇险频率	R11		
.6 叙述工作频率为 406 MHz 的船舶卫星应急无线电示位标(EPIRB)以及配有频率为 121.5 MHz 可自动导引搜救飞机的无线电示位标	R14		
.7 说明 EPIRB 在漂浮释放后自动启动			
.8 演示 EPIRB 的人工启动和关闭			
.9 说明 EPIRB 应最少可工作 48 小时			
.10 说明卫星应急无线电示位标发射的遇险信号通过极地轨道卫星转发到特定的收信台			
.11 叙述工作频率为 1.6 GHz 的船舶卫星应急无线电示位标(EPIRB)	R15		
.12 叙述供 A1 海区使用的应急无线电示位标(EPIRB)			
技能要求:			
14.3 搜救雷达应答器(SARTs)	R2–Reg. Ⅲ/6.2.2 R12		
.1 说明救生艇筏配备搜救雷达应答器(SARTs)的要求			
.2 叙述搜救雷达应答器(SART)			
.3 说明搜救雷达应答器(SART)的工作频率为 9 GHz			
.4 说明搜救雷达应答器(SART)可人工启动和关闭,可以有自动启动的功能			
.5 说明搜救雷达应答器能在预备状态连续工作 96 小时,而且在预备状态后,雷达在连续接收询问时,能工作 8 小时			

Knowledge, understanding and proficiency	IMO reference	Textbooks, bibliography	Teaching aid
Required performance:			
14.4 Distress signals, signalling equipment and pyrotechnics	R1–Table A-Ⅵ/2-1 R2-Reg. Ⅲ/6.3 Ⅴ/16		A1
Distress signals			
.1 lists various distress signals, including distress flares			
Signalling equipment	R3–Sect. 4.1.5, 4.4.8, 5.1.2		
.2 lists the devices for signalling or attracting attention as: – pyrotechnics – torch suitable for Morse signalling – daylight signalling mirror – whistle – orange sails in open boat – searchlight			
.3 demonstrates how to use the daylight signalling mirror			
.4 states that a copy of the life-saving signals is provided			
Pyrotechnics			
.5 lists the pyrotechnics carried in survival craft			
.6 demonstrates how to operate: – rocket parachute flares – hand flares – buoyant smoke floats	R3– Sect. 3.1 Sect. 3.2 Sect. 3.3		
.7 describes when and how to use each of the pyrotechnics			
.8 states that pyrotechnics should only be used on the instructions of the person in charge of the craft			
.9 states the purpose of distress flares	R2–Reg. Ⅲ/6.3		
15 First aid (2 hours)			
Required performance:	R1–Table A-Ⅵ/2-1		ΘA1
15.1 Resuscitation techniques			
.1 demonstrates on a life-size dummy how to apply mouth-to-mouth or mouth-to-nose respiration			
.2 describes the signs of cardiac arrest			
.3 demonstrates closed-chest cardiac compression on the dummy			
.4 demonstrates how two people combine cardiac compression and mouth-to-mouth respiration			
.5 demonstrates the recovery position for an unconscious person			

知识、理解和熟练	IMO 参考书目	教科书、参考文献	教具
技能要求:			
14.4　遇险信号、信号设备和烟火信号	R1–Table A-Ⅵ/2-1		A1
遇险信号	R2–Reg. Ⅲ/6.3 Ⅴ/16		
.1 列出各种类型的遇险信号,包括闪光信号			
信号设备			
.2 列出发出信号或招引注意的设备: —烟火信号 —电筒,适于发射莫尔斯信号 —日光信号镜 —哨子 —开敞式救生艇的橙红色帆 —探照灯	R3–Sect. 4.1 .5, 4.4.8, 5.1.2		
.3 演示如何使用日光信号镜			
.4 说明应备有一份救生信号表			
烟火信号			
.5 列出救生艇筏配备的烟火信号			
.6 演示如何操作各种烟火信号: —火箭降落伞信号 —手持火焰信号 —浮式烟雾信号	R3– Sect. 3.1 Sect. 3.2 Sect. 3.3		
.7 说明各种烟火信号的使用时机和方法			
.8 说明烟火信号应只在艇筏负责人的指令下使用			
.9 说明使用遇险闪光信号的目的	R2–Reg. Ⅲ/6.3		
15　急救(2 小时)			
技能要求:	R1–Table A-Ⅵ/2-1		A1
15.1　复苏术			
.1 演示在人体模具上如何进行口对口、口对鼻人工呼吸			
.2 叙述心脏停止跳动的表征			
.3 演示在人体模具上进行胸外心脏按压			
.4 演示两人配合进行心脏按压和口对口人工呼吸			
.5 演示失去知觉人员的恢复体位			

Knowledge, understanding and proficiency	IMO reference	Textbooks, bibliography	Teaching aid
Required performance:			
15.2 Use of first-aid kit	R1–Table A-VI/2-1		
.1 lists contents of first-aid kit	R3–Sect. 4.1.5.8,		
.2 describes how to deal with the following aboard a survival craft: – bleeding – fractures – burns – shock	4.4.8.20, 5.1.2.2.9 R5		
.3 describes the cause and signs of frostbite			
.4 describes the treatment of frostbite			
.5 describes the cause of non-freezing cold injury (immersion foot)			
.6 explains how to prevent immersion foot			
.7 describes the treatment of immersion foot			
.8 explains the cause of heat stroke and how to avoid it			
.9 describes the treatment for heat stroke			
.10 describes the treatment for contamination by fuel oil			
16 Drills in launching and recovering boats (3 hours)	R1–Table A-VI/2-1		A1
Required performance:			
.1 acts as an efficient member of a launching crew			
.2 takes charge and allocates duties for launching, handling and recovery			
.3 gives correct orders for launching and boarding the boats, clearing the ship's side and handling and disembarking persons from boats			
.4 prepares and safely launches survival craft and clears the ship's side quickly			
.5 demonstrates the ability to start and operate an in board engine fitted in a partial or fully enclosed lifeboat or rescue boat			
.6 demonstrates the ability to row and steer boats and steer by compass			
.7 acts as coxswain in handling boats under power and oars			
.8 streams a sea-anchor			

知识、理解和熟练	IMO 参考书目	教科书、参考文献	教具
技能要求:			
15.2 急救包的使用	R1–Table A-Ⅵ/2-1		
.1 列出急救包的物品	R3–Sect. 4.1.5.8, 4.4.8.20, 5.1.2.2.9		
.2 叙述在救生艇筏上如何处理下列症状: —出血 —骨折 —烧伤 —休克	R5		
.3 叙述冻伤的原因和表征			
.4 叙述冻伤的治疗			
.5 叙述非冻结性冷伤(浸足病)的原因			
.6 解释浸足病的预防			
.7 解释浸足病的治疗			
.8 解释中暑的原因及如何避免			
.9 叙述中暑的治疗			
.10 叙述人体受燃油沾污的治疗			
16 救生艇释放和回收训练(3 小时)	R1–Table A-Ⅵ/2-1		A1
技能要求:			
.1 发挥一名熟练放艇人员的作用			
.2 负责和分配释放、操纵和回收艇的职责			
.3 正确下达放艇和登艇、驶离船舶、操纵小艇以及艇上人员下艇的指令			
.4 准备和安全释放救生艇并迅速驶离船舶			
.5 演示启动和操作半封闭/全封闭救生艇或救助艇内置艇机的能力			
.6 演示划桨、驾艇和运用罗经驾艇的能力			
.7 发挥艇长作用,能在动力和划桨情况下操纵小艇			
.8 释放海锚			

Knowledge, understanding and proficiency	IMO reference	Textbooks, bibliography	Teaching aid
.9 demonstrates the ability to: –use individual items of lifeboats and rescue boats –rig devices to aid location			
.10 demonstrates the ability to safely recover the boats			
17 Drills in launching liferafts (3 hours)	R1–Table A-Ⅵ/2-1		A1
Required performance:			
17.1 Davit-launched liferafts			
.1 acts as an efficient member of a launching crew			
.2 takes charge and allocates duties for launching			
.3 gives correct orders for swinging out the raft, securing it and boarding			
.4 lowers a liferaft			
.5 operates the safety catch of the lifting hook at the correct time			
.6 recovers the hook ready for the next launch			
.7 clears away from ship's side and streams a sea-anchor			
Required performance:			
17.2 Throw-overboard liferafts			
.1 checks that the painter is securely fastened to a strong point or to the hydrostatic release unit (where fitted)			
.2 releases the liferaft manually			
.3 throws the liferaft into the water and hauls in the slack of the painter, causing the raft to inflate			
.4 boards the liferaft and explains how to get clear of ship's side			
Required performance:			
17.3 Boarding a liferaft from the water			
.1 dons a lifejacket/immersion suit correctly, without assistance, within a period of 1 minute			
.2 jumps into the water from a height while wearing a lifejacket/immersion suit			
.3 uses the attached whistle			
.4 demonstrates the "heat-escape-lessening posture" (HELP)			
.5 rights an inverted liferaft			
.6 boards a liferaft from the water while wearing a life jacket			

知识、理解和熟练	IMO 参考书目	教科书、 参考文献	教具
.9 演示以下方面的能力: —使用救生艇和救助艇的各种设备 —安放协助定位的装置			
.10 演示安全收回救生艇的能力			
17 释放救生筏的训练(3小时)	R1–Table A-Ⅵ/2-1		A1
技能要求:			
17.1 吊放式救生筏			
.1 发挥一名熟练放筏人员的作用			
.2 负责和分配放筏职责			
.3 正确下达摆开救生筏、固定和登筏的指令			
.4 放下救生筏			
.5 在适当时候操作救生筏吊钩的安全扣			
.6 收回吊钩准备释放其他救生筏			
.7 离开船舶,释放海锚			
技能要求:			
17.2 投放式救生筏			
.1 检查首缆安全地系在牢固的位置或静水压力释放器上(若装有)			
.2 人工释放救生筏			
.3 将救生筏投入水中,拉紧松弛的拉绳,促使救生筏充气			
.4 登上救生筏和解释如何驶离船舶			
技能要求:			
17.3 水中登救生筏			
.1 在没有协助的情况下,1分钟内正确穿着救生衣或救生服			
.2 在穿着救生衣或救生服的情况下,从高处跳入水中			
.3 使用系在救生衣上的哨子			
.4 演示“减少热量散发的姿势”(HELP)			
.5 扶正倾覆的救生筏			
.6 在穿着救生衣的情况下,从水中登筏			

Knowledge, understanding and proficiency	IMO reference	Textbooks, bibliography	Teaching aid
.7 assists an exhausted survivor to board a liferaft			
.8 throws the rescue quoit and line to a person in the water			
Required performance:			
17.4 Righting an inverted liferaft		R1–Table A-VI/2-1	
.1 rights an inverted liferaft while wearing a lifejacket/immersion suit			
18 Drills in launching and recovering rescue boats (3 hours)			
Required performance:			
.1 acts as an efficient member of a launching crew			
.2 takes charge and allocates duties for launching, handling and recovery			
.3 gives correct commands for launching and boarding the rescue boats, clearing the ship's side and handling and disembarking persons from rescue boats			
.4 prepares and safely launches rescue boats and clears the ship's side quickly			
.5 demonstrates the ability to install, start, operate and safely remove and stow an outboard engine in a rescue boat			
.6 demonstrates the ability to row and steer the rescue boat and to steer by compass			
.7 acts as coxswain in handling rescue boats under power and oars			
.8 streams a sea-anchor			
.9 picks up a survivor from the water			
.10 places a survivor in a stretcher			
.11 safely brings rescue boats alongside			
.12 demonstrates the ability to safely disembark the survivor			
.13 uses foul weather strop for recovery of rescue boats			
19 Practical exercises and evaluation (6 hours)			A1

知识、理解和熟练	IMO 参考书目	教科书、参考文献	教具
.7 协助筋疲力尽的求生者登筏			
.8 向入水者投抛救生浮圈和浮索			
技能要求:			
17.4 扶正倾覆的救生筏	R1–Table A-Ⅵ/2-1		
.1 在穿着救生衣或防水救生服的情况下,扶正水中倾覆的救生筏			
18 释放和回收救助艇的训练(3小时)			
技能要求:			
.1 发挥一名熟练放艇人员的作用			
.2 负责和分配释放、操纵和回收救助艇的职责			
.3 正确下达释放和登艇、驶离船舶、操纵小艇、人员下艇的指令			
.4 准备和安全释放救助艇以及驶离船舶			
.5 演示安装、启动、操作、安全拆除和安放救助艇外置艇机的能力			
.6 演示划桨、驾驶救助艇和运用罗经驾艇的能力			
.7 发挥艇长的作用,在动力和划桨的情况下操纵小艇			
.8 释放海锚			
.9 从水中救起求生者			
.10 将求生者放置在担架上			
.11 救助艇的安全靠泊			
.12 演示求生者安全下艇的能力			
.13 使用恶劣天气回收索回收救助艇			
19 实操训练和评估(6小时)			A1

Part D: Instructor Manual

Introduction

The instructor manual provides guidance on the material that is to be presented during the course. The course material reflects the requirements for the issue of certificates of proficiency in survival craft and rescue boats other than fast rescue boats, as specified in regulation VI/2 of the International Convention on Standards of Training, Certification and Watchkeeping for Seafarers, 1978 as amended in 1995.

The material has been arranged under nineteen main headings:

1 Introduction and safety
2 General
3 Abandon ship
4 Survival craft and rescue boats
5 Launching arrangements
6 Evacuation and recovery of survival craft and rescue boats
7 Actions to take when clear of the ship
8 Lifeboat engine and accessories
9 Rescue boat outboard engine
10 Handling survival craft and rescue boats in rough weather
11 Actions to take when aboard a survival craft
12 Methods of helicopter rescue
13 Hypothermia
14 Radio equipment
15 First aid
16 Drills in launching and recovering boats
17 Drills in launching liferafts
18 Drill in launching and recovering rescue boats
19 Practical exercises and evaluation

The consolidated text of the 1974 SOLAS Convention and the 1978 SOLAS Protocol and amendments (R2) and the International Life-Saving Appliance Code (R3) are used as a basic reference throughout the course. Reference is particularly made to those sections which directly concern the person in charge of the survival craft.

The course outline and timetable provide guidance on the time allocation for the course material, but the instructor is free to make adjustments as necessary. The practical exercises in launching and recovery of boats, allowing each trainee to be in charge of the operation, are very time-demanding. If facilities and instructors are available, the class may be split into two groups to reduce the overall time needed for these exercises. Where that is not possible, the number admitted to the course should be set at a level which will allow each trainee sufficient time in charge. Alternatively, the course could be extended, allowing more time for the final exercises and evaluation, to accommodate a larger number of trainees.

D部分:教员手册

介绍

教员手册为教学过程中所需的课程资料提供指导。课程资料反映了经1995年修正案修订的《1978年海员培训、发证和值班标准国际公约》第Ⅵ/2条规定的关于签发精通救生艇筏和除快速救助艇外的救助艇证书的要求。

课程资料按照以下19个主要标题编排:

1 介绍和安全须知
2 一般要求
3 弃船
4 救生艇筏和救助艇
5 释放装置
6 撤离和救生艇筏、救助艇的回收
7 驶离船舶时应采取的行动
8 救生艇机器及其附属设备
9 救助艇的外置艇机
10 恶劣海况下救生艇筏和救助艇的操纵
11 在救生艇筏上应采取的行动
12 直升机的营救方法
13 体温过低
14 无线电设备
15 急救
16 释放和回收救生艇训练
17 释放救生筏训练
18 释放和回收救助艇训练
19 实操训练和评估

1974年SOLAS公约及1978年SOLAS公约议定书和修正案(R2)和国际救生设备规则(R3)的统一文本,是整个课程的基本参考资料。其中,为那些与负责救生艇筏的人员直接相关的章节提供特别的参考资料。

虽然课程概要和时间表为课程资料提供了时间分配的指导，但教员可自行根据需要进行适当的调整。释放和回收救生艇的实操训练,要求每一个学员进行一次操作是非常费时的。如有足够的设施和教员,可将学员分为两组进行训练以减少课程的总时间。若条件不允许,应控制开班学员的数量,以便使每一个学员有足够的时间进行此类操作;还可以延长课程,在最终训练和评估环节中安排更多的时间,以便容纳更多的学员。

The detailed teaching syllabus must be studied carefully and lesson plans or lecture notes compiled where appropriate. An example of a lesson plan is given on page 92.

Instruction should be made as practical as possible and actual equipment should be used, where available, to illustrate lessons in the classroom. To illustrate the range of boats and davit types, photographs, manufacturers' drawings, videos or models can be used.

Intending trainees should be advised to bring with them a suitable change of clothes, including suitable footwear, for use in wet drills with liferafts and in other practical sessions.

须仔细研究教学大纲细则的内容,编写适当的授课提纲或讲稿。教案的样本见93页。

授课应尽可能切合实际,如有可能应使用真实设备在课堂上进行演示。可以利用图片、制造商的图纸、录像和模型说明救生艇的分类和吊艇架的类型。

应告知受训学员携带适合的更换衣物,包括合适的鞋子,以便在救生筏水中训练和其他实操环节中使用。

Guidance Notes

1 Introduction and safety 0.5 hour

1.1 Introduction

Trainees should be given a brief description of the course and how it will be conducted. They should be advised what clothing to wear for the wet drills and practical sessions, and be informed of arrangements for changing.

1.2 Safety guidance

The chief instructor should explain the safety rules to be followed by trainees during practical sessions. He should also explain the measures taken by instructors for the safety of trainees and how to attract attention if they are in difficulties. On hearing the order "STILL" issued by the trainee in charge of an operation or by an instructor, everything should be stopped and trainees should keep quiet and listen for further instructions. When ready to continue, the order "CARRY ON" should be given.

2 General 1.5 hours

2.1 Emergency situations

Types of emergency
Emphasis should be on the particular problems or difficulties which may be encountered in the various emergency situations. In the case of a fire that threatens to damage survival craft, they should be launched to preserve them. If possible, liferafts should be moved to a safe place on board or placed in the boats in their containers, so that they can be returned on board ready for use if abandonment is unnecessary. They can be launched and inflated from the boat should it be necessary to abandon the ship.

Muster list
A specimen muster list should be used to illustrate this section. Trainees should draw up a muster list for the class as a boat's crew; this list can be used later in the practical exercises.

2.2 Training, drills and operational readiness

The instructor should remind trainees that they are training to act as the person in charge of a survival craft and as such they will be responsible for ensuring that their own crews are familiar with their duties.

A training manual should be available for this session, preferably based on the equipment fitted at the training establishment. Trainees should have access to a copy of the manual throughout the course.

指导说明

1　介绍与安全须知　0.5小时

1.1　介绍

应为学员对课程内容和课程的安排进行简要的描述，建议他们在水上训练和实操环节中应穿何种衣物,告知他们换衣安排。

1.2　安全须知

主讲教员应向学员说明实操期间应遵守的安全操作规程,同时说明为保证学员的安全,教员所采取的措施和学员遇到困难时引起教员注意的方法。当听到负责操作的学员或教员发出“停止”的指令时,应停止手中的一切工作并保持肃静以便听从进一步的指令。当准备继续训练时,应得到“继续”的指令。

2　一般要求　1.5小时

2.1　紧急情况

紧急情况的种类

应强调在各种紧急情况下可能遇到的特殊问题或困难。在一旦发生火灾,会对救生艇筏造成损坏威胁时,应释放救生艇筏加以保护。如可能,应将救生筏存放在容器内并转移到船上安全地点或存放在救生艇中,以便在无须弃船时搬回船上备用。同时在需要弃船时可从救生艇上释放和充气。

应变部署表

利用应变部署表样本进行实例讲解。学员应把班级成员当成艇上船员拟订一份应变部署表;该表可在课程的实操训练时使用。

2.2　训练、演练和良好的操作状态

教员应提醒学员他们被训练担任救生艇筏的指挥人员，为此他们应负责保证自己的船员熟悉各自的职责。

进行本节训练时,应有一份训练手册,其最好能基于该培训机构所安装的设备。学员应能够在本课程中使用该训练手册。

2.3 Actions to be taken when called to survival craft stations

In some ships there may be standing instructions to lower boats to embarkation deck level as soon as the crew is assembled. The boats in new cargo ships musts be capable of being boarded and launched from the stowed position. In passenger ships, boats can be boarded either at the stowed position or at an embarkation deck, but not both.

3 Abandon ship 0.5 hour

Actions to be taken when required to abandon ship
The fastening of safety belts in free-fall boats is essential. An unfastened occupant will be thrown when the boat strikes the water and may seriously injure both himself and other occupants.

Totally enclosed boats depend for their self-righting properties on the occupants remaining securely in place when capsized.

Supervision of boarding liferafts through marine evacuation system may be demonstrated through the videos 'Viking Marine Escape Slide' (V13) and 'Viking Marine Evacuation System' (V14).

4 Survival craft and rescue boats 0.75 hour

The boats and liferafts to be used in practical drills should be used to demonstrate the construction and fittings. Photographs, drawings or videos of other types of boats should be used.

5 Launching arrangements 1.25 hours

This section could well be dealt with at the same time as Section 4. For example, a particular type of survival craft and its launching arrangements could be treated together.

The subsection on marine evacuation system is covered in video cassettes V13 and V14.

Trainees should be warned that hydrostatic release units should not be painted. Paint may block the holes through which water must enter to operate the release.

6 Evacuation and recovery of survival craft and rescue boats 1.25 hours

Subject areas 6.1 and 6.2 are in preparation for the practical exercises in launching and clearing the ship's side. Bowsing-in tackles and tracing pendants are not fitted to boats which are launched from the stowed position.

In objective 6.3.2 a motor lifeboat or rescue boat should be used.

2.3 召集到救生艇站时的行动

在一些船上,常规指令是一旦船员集合后立即放下救生艇至登艇甲板位置。新造货船的救生艇必须能够从存放位置登艇和释放。在客船上,救生艇应能够在存放位置登艇或在登艇甲板登艇,但两者不可兼得。

3 弃船 0.5小时

弃船时应采取的行动

在自由降落式救生艇内系好安全带至关重要。当救生艇撞击水面时,没有系好安全带的乘员将被抛起,并可能造成自身和其他艇员的严重伤害。

全封闭式救生艇倾覆时,其自扶性能取决于乘员是否紧紧地保持在原来的位置。

对经海上撤离系统登上救生筏的监控可通过录像片"维京海上逃生滑道"(V13)和"维京海上撤离系统"(V14)进行演示。

4 救生艇筏和救助艇 0.75小时

在实操训练中,使用救生艇和救生筏来展示其结构及属具。其他类型救生艇的图片、图纸或录像应予以采用。

5 艇筏释放装置 1.25小时

本节的内容应与第4节完全同步进行。例如,一个特定的救生艇筏及其释放装置应结合在一起同时讲解。

海上撤离系统部分的有关内容包含在录像带V13和V14中。

应告诫学员救生筏的静水力释放装置不应上油漆。油漆可能阻塞让海水进入启动释放装置的孔洞。

6 撤离和回收救生艇筏、救助艇 1.25小时

科目6.1和6.2是关于释放和驶离船舶方面实操训练的准备项目。从存放位置释放救生艇时,不要装上止荡索和定位索。

在目标6.3.2中应使用机动救生艇和救助艇。

The instructor should impress on trainees that an inflatable liferaft, even when a sea-anchor is streamed, will drift faster than a survivor can swim. A person who has hold of a liferaft should never let go of it and anyone entering the water to assist another person must have a line attached so that he can be pulled back to the raft.

Launching survival craft and rescue boats in rough weather
A ship stopped in a high wind will probably lie with the wind approximately abeam and will drift quite rapidly to leeward. Survival craft, particularly liferafts, will experience difficulty in getting clear of the lee side and will probably be dependent on a motor lifeboat or rescue boat to tow them clear.

On the weather side, conditions will be much rougher and it will be difficult to hold craft alongside for boarding. Streaming a sea-anchor will slow the drift of survival craft sufficiently to allow the ship to drift away from them.

When beaching in deserted or remote areas, efforts should be made to save the survival craft and its equipment. They will continue to be useful for shelter and much of the equipment can be put to use, particularly the means of attracting attention and, of course, the food and water.

7 Actions to take when clear of the ship 0.25 hour

The instructor should stress the need to quickly get away from a sinking ship to avoid violent local suction due to foundering. Every attempt, however, shall be made to pick up survivors and other items of use floating in the water.

8 Lifeboat engine and accessories 1.5 hours

The instruction should be made as practical as possible, using the engine in the lifeboat or a workshop. Details of operating procedures and maintenance for the engines installed in a ship's lifeboats are contained in the training manual and instructions for on-board maintenance. Starting and operating instructions are also mounted near the engine starting controls.

Trainees should be aware of the amount of fuel carried, to enable them to plan its use to best advantage.

9 Rescue boat outboard engine 1 hour

The instructions should be made as practical as possible. Details of securing, priming, starting, throttling and stopping the engine should be demonstrated using an outboard engine and a waterdrum.

10 Handling survival craft and rescue boats in rough weather 0.75 hour

It should be explained to trainees that short choppy seas will inevitably lead to a "wet" ride in the rescue boats. The pounding of the hull and resultant vibrations can lead to the crew becoming injured. Great care is needed until craft arrive in a safe area.

Use of oil bags and a sea-anchor should be made to heave-to in heavy seas and swell.

教员应使学员铭记:即使在释放海锚时,气胀式救生筏的漂流速度比求生者游泳速度要快。抓住救生筏的人员千万不要放开,而下水协助其他人员的任何人都必须系上绳索以便可以将他拉回到救生筏上。

恶劣海况下释放救生艇筏和救助艇

在强风中船舶将很可能保持在与风向大约正横的位置,并以相当快的速度向下风漂移。救生艇筏,特别是救生筏,在驶离船舶下风侧时将遇到困难,并很可能依靠机动救生艇或救助艇拖离。

在船舶上风侧,海况将会更加恶劣,这将难以使艇筏系固和登艇。流放海锚将极大地减慢救生艇筏的漂流速度,使船舶漂离救生艇筏。

在荒凉或偏僻的地区抢滩时,应尽一切努力保存救生艇筏及其设备。救生艇筏可用于人员的遮蔽,许多设备可以拿来使用,特别是招引注意的设备,当然还包括食品和淡水。

7 驶离船舶时应采取的行动 0.25小时

教员应强调的是:必须尽快远离正在沉没的船舶,以避开由于沉没所产生的强大的局部吸力。然而无论如何应尽一切努力打捞漂浮在水中的求生者和其他有用的物品。

8 救生艇机和艇上附属器具 1.5小时

教学应尽可能结合实际,使用救生艇上或车间里的机器进行授课。在训练手册和船上维护保养须知中要含有与安装在船舶救生艇上的机器的操作程序和维护保养有关的详细资料。启动和操作说明书通常也存放于机器启动控制板附近。

学员应知道艇上燃油的装运数量,使他们能够最有利地安排使用。

9 救助艇外置艇机 1小时

本节的教学应尽可能结合实际。使用外挂艇机和水桶演示讲解艇机的系固、燃油添加、机器的启动、调速和停止的详细情况。

10 恶劣海况下救生艇筏和救助艇筏的操纵 0.75小时

应向学员解释说明汹涌的波涛将不可避免地导致上浪并弄湿救助艇。海浪对艇体的拍击和合成振动可导致船员受伤。应加倍小心直到艇筏到达安全海域。

在大风浪和强涌时应施放使用镇浪油袋和海锚以稳住救生艇筏。

11 Actions to take when aboard a survival craft 1.5 hours

In objective 11.1.6, the order in which the actions would be taken would depend upon circumstances; some of them could be taken simultaneously. If the survival craft are all secured together, only one EPIRB should be activated. The other one should be activated after 48 hours, when the first will be reaching the end of its transmission capability.

A watch system should be organised, giving some duty to each occupant of a survival craft. Having something to do or to be responsible for improves the morale of individual survivors and of the group in general. A constant lookout should be maintained, changing the lookout at about 2 hourly intervals or less in cold conditions, or if there is a danger of sunburn. Lookouts should be instructed to keep watch all round the horizon and to listen as well as watch. They should be alert for signs of ships, aircraft, land, dangers and rain showers, which may provide an opportunity to supplement the water ration. On making any sighting, the lookout should inform the person in charge of the craft before doing anything else.

Complete sets of lifeboat and liferaft equipment should be available for demonstration. For the equipment which is dealt with fully elsewhere, reference should be made to its stowage in the survival craft.

When apportioning water, it should be remembered that survivors suffering from shock, after burns or loss of blood for example, will need more water than the recommended 0.5 litre per day to keep them alive.

12 Methods of helicopter rescue 1.25 hours

Procedures for rescue from the ship, from survival craft and from the water should be covered. Search and rescue helicopters are mostly equipped to communicate on VHF channel 16, which allows direct communication between the helicopter and a ship or a survival craft carrying a portable two-way radiotelephone. Each trainee should demonstrate how to don a rescue sling and signal that he is ready to be lifted.

In all cases it is important to try to follow any instructions from the helicopter crew as closely as possible.

13 Hypothermia 1 hour

In many cases this is the most likely condition which will need recognition and treatment, particularly with survivors who have been immersed before boarding a survival craft. A Pocket Guide to Cold Water Survival (R5) deals with the avoidance and treatment of hypothermia.

11　在救生艇筏上应采取的行动　1.5小时

在学习目标11.1.6中,应采取的行动的指令将根据环境决定;许多行动可同时进行。如果所有救生艇筏绑扎系固在一起,应只启用一个应急无线电示位标。其他的示位标应在48小时以后当第一个示位标到其发射能力的极限时使用。

应组织建立艇上的值班制度,给救生艇筏每个乘员分配一些职责,让他们有事做或负责某件事,会提高个人求生者和团体的整体士气。应保持连续瞭望,约每2小时轮换瞭望人员,在寒冷的天气条件下或有日灼危险时应适当缩短轮换时间。应指示瞭望人员注意水平线四周的瞭望,同时采取听觉瞭望。瞭望人员应注意船舶、飞机、陆地、危险的迹象和可能提供水量补充机会的阵雨。一旦发现任何迹象,在采取行动之前,瞭望人员应立即通知艇筏的负责人。

应备有一整套的救生艇和救生筏的设备供教学演示。对完全在其他位置操控的设备,在救生艇筏上应注明其存放位置。

在分配淡水时,应记住:出现休克(例如烧伤或失血后)的求生者需要比推荐的每天0.5升的水量更多的水以维持生命。

12　直升机营救方法　1.25小时

应包含从船上、从救生艇筏上和从水中营救人员的程序。搜救直升机大部分都装有VHF CH16频道的通信设备,可在直升机与船舶或备有手提式双向无线电话的救生艇筏之间进行直接通信。每位学员应能演示如何穿上直升机救生吊绳和备妥待吊的信号。

在任何情况下都应尽可能地严格执行直升机机组人员的指令是非常重要的。

13　体温过低　1小时

在许多情况下,这是需要诊断和治疗的最可能的一种情况,特别是对上救生艇筏前已经过水中浸泡的求生者。《冷水中求生指南》袖珍本(R5)述及体温过低的避免和治疗。

14 Radio equipment 1.5 hours

The amendments to SOLAS 1974 regulation III/6, "Communications", entered into force on 1 January 1998. The regulation stipulates that all passenger ships and cargo ships of 500 gross tonnage and upwards will require at least three portable two-way VHF radiotelephones and, in addition, a radar transponder on each side of the ship, stowed so that they can be rapidly placed in any survival craft other than the additional liferaft or liferafts that must be carried when the survival craft are more than 100 metres from the stem or stern. Cargo ships of 300 gross tonnage and upwards but less than 500 tons will require at least two portable two-way VHF radiotelephones and one radar transponder.

Lifeboats may have fixed two-way VHF radiotelephones fitted. The requirements for radar transponders may be met by having a transponder stowed in each survival craft, in which case they would replace the radar reflectors required under the existing rules.

The radar transponder is triggered by radar pulses in the 9 GHz band(3 cm wavelength) to transmit a signal showing as a row of dots on the display of the radar which triggered it. An audible or visual signal will indicate to survivors that the transponder has been triggered. Distress alerting will be carried out by the ship's satellite EPIRB, which would be transferred to a survival craft on abandoning the ship.

Survival craft EPIRBs may not be activated by being placed in the water; they must be manually activated. Ship's float-free satellite EPIRBs operating on 406 MHz are automatically activated when in the water and can also be manually activated and deactivated. No transmission should be possible from the EPIRB used for demonstration purposes.

Signalling equipment and pyrotechnics
A set of dummy pyrotechnics should be available for demonstration purposes. Only a small number of pyrotechnics is carried, so it is important that trainees know when to use them effectively and do not waste them in circumstances where they are unlikely to be seen.

15 First-aid 2 hours

15.1 Resuscitation techniques

Trainees should have undertaken a course in basic first aid which included resuscitation early in their sea-going careers. This section should be treated as an opportunity to check that they can still apply the methods correctly. Some trainees should be asked to demonstrate resuscitation in the crowded and confined space of a survival craft, which need not be afloat for this exercise.

15.2 Use of first-aid kit

The contents of a first-aid kit and how they can be used to treat injuries likely to be sustained by survivors are dealt with in this section. Treatments should be confined to what is possible in a survival craft and the equipment to hand.

14 无线电设备 1.5小时

SOLAS 1974修正案第III/6条“通信”于1998年1月1日实施。该条规定:所有客船和500总吨及以上的货船应配备至少3只手提式双向VHF无线电话。另外,在两边船舷各配一个雷达应答器,以便能够快速地放置在任何救生艇筏上,不包括救生艇筏离开船头或船尾超过100米时而需另外配备的救生筏。300总吨及以上但未满500总吨的货船要求配备至少2只手提式双向VHF无线电话和1只雷达应答器。

救生艇可装备固定式双向VHF无线电设备。在每只救生艇上安放一只雷达应答器可满足对雷达应答器的要求。此种做法下,雷达应答器可取代在现行规则中规定配备的雷达反射器。

雷达应答器被9 GHz频带(3cm波长)的雷达脉冲信号触发而发射信号,该发射信号在引起触发的雷达显示器上显示成一串圆点。一种听觉或视觉信号会告知求生者应答器已被触发。应使用船上的应急卫星无线电示位标(EPIRB)发射遇险信号,在弃船时应将应急无线电示位标转移到救生艇筏上。

救生艇筏应急无线电示位标(EPIRBs)放入水中不会被激活启动,它必须由人工启动。工作频率为 406 MHz 的船舶自浮释放式卫星应急无线电示位标(EPIRBs)在水中时将被自动激活启动,同时也可采取人工方式启动和关闭。不能为教学演示的目的而触发应急无线电示位标。

信号设备和烟火信号

应备有一套仿制烟火信号供教学示范。船上仅备有少量的烟火信号,因此让学员懂得何时有效地使用烟火信号以及在不太可能被发现时避免浪费烟火就显得大为重要。

15 急救 2小时

15.1 复苏术

学员在海上职业生涯的最初阶段就已接受过包括人工呼吸在内的基本急救课程的培训。本节应视为一个检查他们是否还能正确使用此方法的机会。应要求部分学员演示在救生艇筏上的拥挤和有限空间进行人工呼吸,但不要求在漂浮状态下做此训练。

15.2 急救包的使用

本节讲解的内容是:急救包的物品和如何使用它们治疗求生者很可能遭受的伤害。治疗的范围应限制在救生艇筏上可进行的和现有设备的范围内。

Survivors may be affected by oil on the water when abandoning ship, which will result in some or all of the following:

- swallowing oil
- oil covering the skin and clothes
- inhalation of oil into the lungs
- inflammation of the eyes

Swallowed oil will cause vomiting, and the sufferer should be given additional water. Oil should be wiped off the skin with anything available in the survival craft. A complete covering of oil, preventing perspiration, can prove fatal if not cleaned off. Clothes can be trailed in the water to remove as much oil as possible. Eyes should be washed out and protected from bright sunlight as far as possible until the inflammation has gone. Inhaled oil prevents efficient oxygen exchange in the lungs and may lead to pneumonia, but there is little that can be done for a victim in a survival craft.

16 Drills in launching and recovering boats 3 hours

The trainees will act as members of the boat's crew or passengers for the drills. Use should be made of the muster list drawn up on the first morning. Each trainee should take charge of a launching operation and clear the boat away from alongside. A trainee's duties will be changed to cover all items in the muster list in the course of the drills.

Each trainee should also take a turn as coxswain to practise handling the boat, including coming alongside for recovery of the boat.

The sea anchor should be streamed and recovered at some point during the practises to ensure that trainees know what is involved.

In one or two of the drills, the evacuation of a stretcher case should be practised. The Neil-Robertson stretcher should be padded and weighted to represent the casualty.

17 Drills in launching liferafts 3 hours

Trainees should be warned to wear their change of clothes for a wet drill and the instructor should check that their footwear will not damage the liferafts.

Abandon ship drills should be held, using both a davit-launched and hand-launched liferaft.

Boarding a davit-launched liferaft, the positioning of occupants, the release of the safety catch and the automatic release of the hook on romoval of the load can be exercised by suspending the raft at a small height above the deck or platform adjacent to the davit and lowering it on to the deck.

Positioning a stretcher casualty should be included in one of the boarding drills.

Finally, the liferaft should be launched and cleared away from the side by the crew, using paddles and a suitably weighted sea-anchor. Trainees should be instructed to try to board the liferaft dry. It will almost certainly be necessary to tow the liferaft back with the boat; the securing and towing should form part of the exercise.

It is recommended that all trainees are made to jump into the water from a height of at least 4.5 m, wearing a lifejacket, during an abandon ship drill with a hand-launched liferaft. For that reason it is advisable to make it the final drill of the day.

弃船时,求生者可能受水中浮油的伤害导致下列部分或全部结果:

—咽下油料
—皮肤和衣物沾满油
—将油吸入肺部
—眼部发炎

咽下油料将引起呕吐,受害者应被给予额外的淡水。皮肤沾油时应用救生艇筏上的任何可用物品擦除;全身沾满油料会阻止皮肤排汗,如不清除会有生命危险。可将衣物在水中拖曳以尽可能地清除油渍。眼睛须进行彻底清洗并尽可能防止阳光照射,直到炎症消除。吸入油料会阻碍肺内充分的氧气交换并可能导致肺炎,但在救生艇筏上治疗患者的措施很有限。

16　救生艇释放和回收训练　3小时

学员应作为救生艇乘员或旅客参与训练。使用第一天课程中草拟的应变部署表。每一位学员都应负责救生艇释放和驶离船舶的操作。在实操训练中学员应轮换职责以覆盖应变部署表的所有操作项目。

每一位学员还应轮流担任艇长以练习救生艇的操纵,包括靠上船旁回收救生艇。

在训练期间，应在一些地点进行海锚的释放和回收操作，确保学员了解该操作所涉及的内容。

在所进行一到两次训练中,应安排进行担架重伤员的撤离训练,应填充和加重尼尔-罗勃逊(Neil-Robertson)担架以代表伤亡人员。

17　释放救生筏训练　3小时

教员应提醒学员换上备用衣物进行湿式训练,并检查学员的鞋子不至于损坏救生筏。

应举行弃船训练,吊架释放式和手动释放式救生筏两种方式都要使用。

登上吊架释放式救生筏,乘员就位;在失去负载情况下脱开安全扣和进行自动脱钩训练,可通过在甲板上或吊架附近的平台上低高度悬挂救生筏,然后降落救生筏至甲板来实现。

在其中一次登筏训练中应进行一次担架重伤员就位的训练。

最后,由船员释放救生筏并驶离船旁,使用划桨和合适重量的海锚。应指示学员尝试保持自身干燥地登上救生筏。用救助艇拖回救生筏肯定是需要的;因此固定和拖带也应是训练的一部分。

建议在使用人力释放式救生筏进行弃船训练中,所有学员训练时都穿着救生衣,从至少4.5米高的地点跳入水中。鉴于上述原因,建议将该项训练作为当天最后一个项目。

Trainees should use the whistle, swim a short distance, right an inverted liferaft, board the liferaft from water and once on board help others to board the liferaft. When ready to clear away from the side, the instructor can let go of the painter instead of having it cut at the raft. As with the previous exercise, the safety boat will be needed to bring the liferaft back.

The rescue boat should be kept on stand-by to help and in towing the liferaft back.

18 Drills in launching and recovering rescue boats 3 hours

The trainees will act as members of rescue boat crews for the drills. Each trainee should take charge of a launching operation and clear the rescue boats away from alongside. A trainee's duties will be changed to cover all items of rescue boats' crew.

Each trainee should take turns to act as coxswain to practise boat handling, including coming alongside for recovery of rescue boats.

The sea anchor should be streamed and recovered at some point during the practise.

Practise drills for picking up survivors in water should be carried out with emphasis on recovery in horizontal posture. In one or two drills, the evacuation of a stretcher case should be practised. The Neil-Robertson stretcher should be padded and weighted to represent the casualty.

Finally, the recovery of rescue boats should be carried out with the help of foul weather strops, demonstrating the transfer of the weight of boat between the strop and fall wire.

19 Practical exercises and evaluation 6 hours

The final day should be used to complete the drills in launching and recovering survival craft and rescue boats, started in subject area 16, and for evaluation of trainees. The time spent on this section should be extended if necessary.

Evaluation should be based mainly on the trainees' performance in practical exercises. Before issue of a course document, a trainee must demonstrate proficiency in the operations of survival craft and rescue boats that are specified in column 3 of Table A-VI/2-1 of the STCW Code.

In evaluating proficiency, special consideration should be given to the trainee's ability to:

(a) understand and carry out, promptly and correctly, the orders and instructions of the person in charge of an operation;

(b) co-ordinate his actions with those of other members of the crew;

(c) take charge of boarding, launching and clearing away from the side with confidence, controlling the operation with timely and clear commands; and

(d) manage a survival craft afloat, and in the case of a boat, manoeuvre it as required.

The minimum standard of competence required for the issue of certificates of proficiency in survival craft is contained in column 1 of Table A-VI/2-1 of the STCW Code.

学员应使用口哨,进行短距离游泳,扶正倾覆的救生筏,从水中登筏并在登筏后协助其他人员登筏。当准备好驶离船舶时,教员可松开救生筏艏缆以代替砍断它。正如以前的训练一样,需要用安全救助艇将救生筏带回。

救助艇应随时保持待命,准备救助和拖回救生筏。

18　释放和回收救助艇的训练　3小时

学员应作为救助艇乘员或旅客参与训练。每一位学员都应学会救生艇释放和驶离船舶的操作。在实操训练中,学员应轮换职责以覆盖救助艇乘员的所有操作项目。

每一位学员还应轮流担任艇长以练习救助艇的操纵,包括靠上船旁回收救助艇。

在训练期间,应在同一位置进行流放和回收海锚操作。

应进行救捞水中求生者的实操训练并把侧重点放在以水平姿势救起求生者上, 在其中一到两次训练中应进行担架重伤员的撤离训练,应填充和加重尼尔–罗勃逊(Neil-Robertson)担架以代表伤亡人员。

最后,在恶劣天气带索的协助下进行救助艇的回收训练,并进行在该带索和滑车钢丝绳之间进行救助艇重量转移的演示。

19　实操训练和评估　6小时

最后一天,应从主题范围16开始完成救生艇筏、救助艇的释放和回收综合训练,并对学员进行评估。必要时可延长本节所需的时间。

评估应主要以学员在实操训练中的表现为基础。在签发课程培训证书前,学员必须表明精通STCW规则表A-Ⅵ/2-1第3栏列明的有关救生艇筏和救助艇的操作。

对是否精通的评估,应特别考虑学员的下列能力:

(a)快速、正确地理解和执行负责该项操作人员的指令和指示;
(b)与其他艇员协调行动;
(c)从容地负责登艇、放艇和驶离船舶,控制及时,口令清晰;以及
(d)管理救生艇筏的航行,如果是一艘艇,按要求进行驾驶的能力。

签发精通救生艇筏证书要求的最低适任标准已列在STCW规则表A-Ⅵ/2-1第1栏中。

Example of a Lesson Plan

COURSE: PROFICIENCY IN SURVIVAL CRAFT AND RESCUE BOATS OTHER THAN FAST RESCUE BOATS **LESSON NUMBER:** **DURATION:**15 minutes

Training Area: Actions to take when clear of the ship

KNOWLEDGE, UNDERSTANDING AND PROFICIENCY Required performance(In teaching sequence with memory keys)	TEACHING METHOD	IMO REFERENCE	A/V AIDS	INSTRUCTOR GUIDELINES	TIME MINS
7 Actions to take when clear of the ship .1 1/4 mile clear of ship: – clear of masts, rigging, flotsam and surfacing wreckage – oil on surface – further off if volatile cargo oil – local suction from ship foundering	*Classroom lecture*	R1 Table.A-VI/2-1 Col.2		A1-Para 7	3
.2 recovery of survivors: – head count – lookout – searchlights and other means – early recovery preferred – recovery in horizontal posture					3
.3 equipment recovery: – safety equipment, viz. SART, EPIRB – other items of use – method of launch and recovery					3
.4 communication: – importance of communication – information exchange between craft – available means of communication – VHF channel to use					3
.5 action by survival craft: – importance of this action – leaks in flotation chambers, distribution of survivors and equipment – help each other in need – plan course of action					3

教案实例

课程: 精通救生艇筏和除快速救助艇外的救助艇　　**课程编号:**　　**授课时间:15分钟**

培训知识点: 驶离船舶时应采取的行动

知识、理解和熟练 技能要求(按教学顺序和记忆要点的顺序)	教学 方法	IMO 参考书目	视听教具	教员 指南	时间 分钟
7　驶离船舶时应采取的行动 .1 驶离船舶1/4海里: —远离桅杆、索具、漂浮货物和露出水面的残骸 —水面浮油,若为挥发性货油,需进一步远离 —沉船的局部吸力	课程讲授	R1 Table.A-Ⅵ/2-1 Col.2		A1-Para 7	3
.2 营救求生者: —清点人数 —瞭望 —探照灯和其他工具 —及早营救 —以水平姿势捞取求生者					3
.3 保全设备: —安全设备,即SART,EPIRB —其他有用物品 —释放和回收方法					3
.4 通信: —通信的重要性 —艇筏之间信息交换 —可用的通信手段 —VHF频道的使用					3
.5 救生艇筏的行动: —行动的重要性 —浮室漏水,求生人员和设备的分配 —帮助需要帮助的人 —计划行动过程					3

Appendix：Table of Life-Saving Signals

1 Landing signals for the guidance of small boats with crews or persons in distress.

	MANUAL SIGNALS	LIGHT SIGNALS	OTHER SIGNALS	SIGNIFICATION
Day signals	**Vertical** motion of a white flag or of the arms	or firing of a **green** star signal	— · — or code letter **K** given by light or sound-signal apparatus	**This is the best place to land**
Night signals	**Vertical** motion of a white light or flare	or firing of a **green** star signal	— · — or code letter **K** given by light or sound-signal apparatus	

A range (indication of direction) may be given by placing a steady white light or flare at a lower level and in line with the observer.

	MANUAL SIGNALS	LIGHT SIGNALS	OTHER SIGNALS	SIGNIFICATION
Day signals	**Horizontal** motion of a white flag or of the arms extended horizontally	or firing of a **red** star signal	· · · or code letter **S** given by light or sound-signal apparatus	**Landing here highly dangerous**
Night signals	**Horizontal** motion of a light or flare	or firing of a **red** star signal	· · · or code letter **S** given by light or sound-signal apparatus	
Day signals	1 **Horizontal** motion of a white flag. followed by 2 the placing of the white flag in the ground and 3 by the carrying of another white flag in the direction to be indicated	1 or firing of a **red** star signal vertically and 2 a **white** star signal in the direction towards the better landing place	1 or signalling the code letter **S**(...) followed by the code letter **R**(·–·) if a better landing place for the craft in distress is located more to the *right* in the direction of approach 2 or signalling the code letter **S**(...) followed by the code letter **L** (·–··) if a better landing place for the craft in distress is located more to the *left* in the direction of approach	**Landing here highly dangerous. A more favourable location for landing is in the direction indicated**
Night signals	1 **Horizontal** motion of a white light. or flare 2 followed by the placing of the white light or flare on the ground and 3 the carrying of another white light or flare in the direction to be indicated	1 or firing of a **red** star signal vertically and a 2 **white** star signal in the direction towards the better landing place	1 or signalling the code letter **S** (...) followed by the code letter **R** (·–·) if a better landing place for the craft in distress is located more to the *right* in the direction of approach 2 or signalling the code letter **S** (...) followed by the code letter **L** (·–··) if a better landing place for the craft in distress is located more to the *left* in the direction of approach	

附录:救生信号表

1　引导载有遇险船员或人员的小艇登陆的信号。

	手操信号	发光信号	其他信号	意义
白天信号	一面白旗或双臂上下挥动	或发射一**绿色**星光信号	或者用灯光或音响信号装置发出字母“K”	这是最好的登陆地点
夜间信号	一盏白灯或火焰上下挥动	或发射一**绿色**星光信号	或者用灯光或音响信号装置发出字母“K”	

可在低处放置一固定的白灯或火焰并与瞭望者成一直线,以此作为示标(指示方向)。

	手操信号	发光信号	其他信号	意义
白天信号	一面白旗或双臂平举做**水平**运动	或发射一**红色**星光信号	或用灯光或音响信号装置发出字母“S”	在此处登陆极危险
夜间信号	一盏白灯或火焰做**水平**运动	或发射一**红色**星光信号	或用灯光或音响信号装置发出字母“S”	
白天信号	1 一面白旗做**水平**运动 2 接着把白旗插在地上并 3 拿另一面指示引导的方向	1 或者垂直地发射一**红色**星光信号并 2 向较好的登陆地点方向发射一**白色**星光信号	如在遇险船舶驶进方向的较偏右侧有较好的登陆地点,发出字母信号“S”(···)接着又发出字母信号“R”(·—·) 如在遇险船舶驶进方向的较偏左侧有较好的登陆地点,发出字母信号“S”(···)接着又发出字母信号“L”(·—··)	在此处登陆极危险。在所指示的方向有较好的登陆地点
夜间信号	1 一盏白灯或者火焰做**水**平运动 2 接着把白灯或者火焰放在地上并 3 拿另一盏白灯或者火焰指示引导的方向	1.或者垂直地发射一**红色**星光信号并 2.向较好的登陆地点方向发射一**白色**星光信号	1 如在遇险船舶驶进方向的较偏右侧有较好的登陆地点,发出字母信号“S”(···)接着又发出字母信号“R”(·—·) 2 如在遇险船舶驶进方向的较偏左侧有较好的登陆地点,发出字母信号“S”(···)接着又发出字母信号“L”(·—··)	

2 Signals to be employed in connection with the use of shore life-saving apparatus.

	MANUAL SIGNALS	LIGHT SIGNALS	OTHER SIGNALS	SIGNIFICATION
Day signals	**Vertical** motion of a white flag or of the arms	or firing of a **green** star signal		**In general: affirmative** **Specifically:rocket line** **Is held-** **tail block is** **made fast-** **hawser is** **made fast-** **man is in the** **breeches buoy-** **haul away**
Night signals	**Vertical** motion of a white light or flare	or firing of a **green** star signal		
Day signals	**Horizontal** motion of a white flag or of the arms extended horizontally	or firing of a **red** star signal		**In general: negative** **Specifically:slack away** **-avast** **hauling**
Night signals	**Horizontal** motion of a white light or flare	or firing of a **red** star signal		

3 Replies from life-saving saving stations or maritime rescue units to distress signals made by a ship or person.

Day signals		Orange smoke signal	or combinde *light* and *sound* signal (thunder-light) consisting of 3 single signals which are fired at intervals of approximately one minute	**You are seen-** **assistance will be given** **as soon as possible** (Repetition of such signal shall have the same meaning)
Night signals		1min 1min **White** star-rocket consisting or 3 single signals which are fired at intervals of approximately one minute		

If necessary, the day signals may be given at night or the night signals by day.

2 使用岸上救生设备时所用的信号。

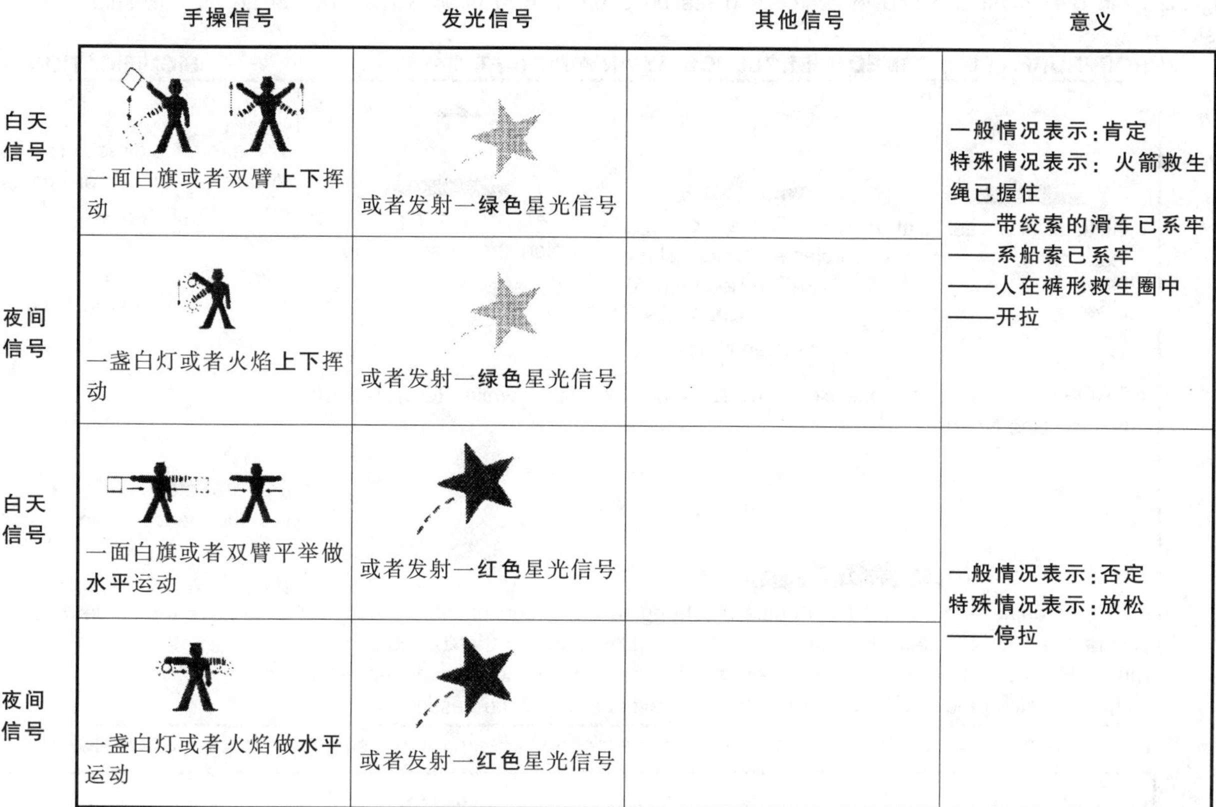

	手操信号	发光信号	其他信号	意义
白天信号	一面白旗或者双臂上下挥动	或者发射一绿色星光信号		一般情况表示:肯定 特殊情况表示:火箭救生绳已握住 ——带绞索的滑车已系牢 ——系船索已系牢 ——人在裤形救生圈中 ——开拉
夜间信号	一盏白灯或者火焰上下挥动	或者发射一绿色星光信号		
白天信号	一面白旗或者双臂平举做水平运动	或者发射一红色星光信号		一般情况表示:否定 特殊情况表示:放松 ——停拉
夜间信号	一盏白灯或者火焰做水平运动	或者发射一红色星光信号		

3 救生站或海事救助单位对船舶或个人所发遇险信号的回答。

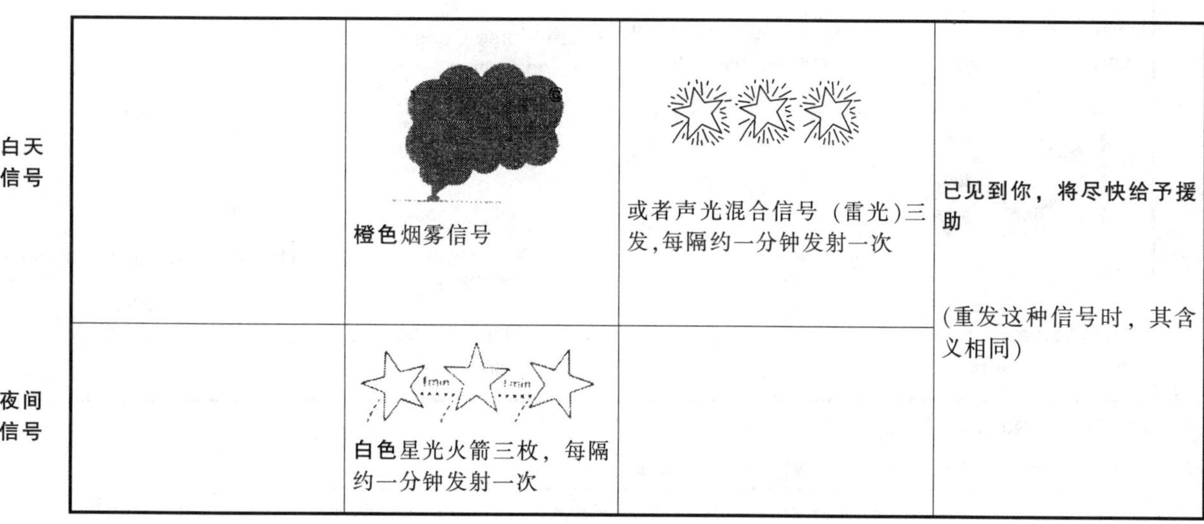

白天信号		橙色烟雾信号	或者声光混合信号(雷光)三发,每隔约一分钟发射一次	已见到你,将尽快给予援助 (重发这种信号时,其含义相同)
夜间信号		白色星光火箭三枚,每隔约一分钟发射一次		

必要时,白天信号可用于夜间或者夜间信号用于白天。

4 Air-to-surface visual signals.

Signals used by aircraft engaged in search and rescue operations to direct ships towards an aircraft, ship or person in distress:

PROCEDURES PERFORMED IN SEQUENCE BY AN AIRCRAFT			SIGNIFICATION
1 CIRCLE the vessel at least once.	2 CROSS the vessel's projected course close AHEAD at a low altitude while ROCKING the wings.(See Note).	3 HEAD in the direction in which the vessel is to be directed.	The aircraft is directing a vessel toward an aircraft or vessel in distress. (Repetition of such signals shall have the same meaning)
4 CROSS the vessel's wake close ASTERN at low altiude while ROCKING the wings. (See Note) NOTE Opening and closing the throttle or changing the propeller pitch may also be practiced as an alternative means of attracting attention to that of rocking the wings. However, this form of sound signal may be less effective than the visual signal of rocking the wings owing to high noise level on board the vessel.			The assistance of the vessel is no longer required. (Repetition of such signals shall have the same meaning)

Signals used by a vessel in response to an aircraft engeged in search and resue operations			SIGNIFICATION
Hoist "Code and Answering" pendant Close up; or	Change the heading to the required direction; or	Flash Morse Code signal "T" by signal lamp.	Acknowledges receipt of aircraft's signal
Hoist international flag "N" (NOVEMBER);or		Flash Morse Code signal "N" by signal lamp.	Indicates inability to comply

5 Surface-to-air visual signals.

Communication from surface craft or survivors to an aircraft.

Use the following surface-to-air visual signals by displaying the appropriate signal on the deck or on the ground

Message	ICAO*/IMO**visual signals
– Require assistance	V
– Require medical assistance	X
– No or negative	N
– Yes or affirmative	Y
– Proceeding in this direction	↑

* ICAO annex 12–Search and rescue.

** IMO SAR AND MERSAR Manuals.

4 空中对水面的可视信号。

飞机在进行搜寻与救助作业中指引船舶驶向遇险的飞机、船舶或人员所使用的信号:

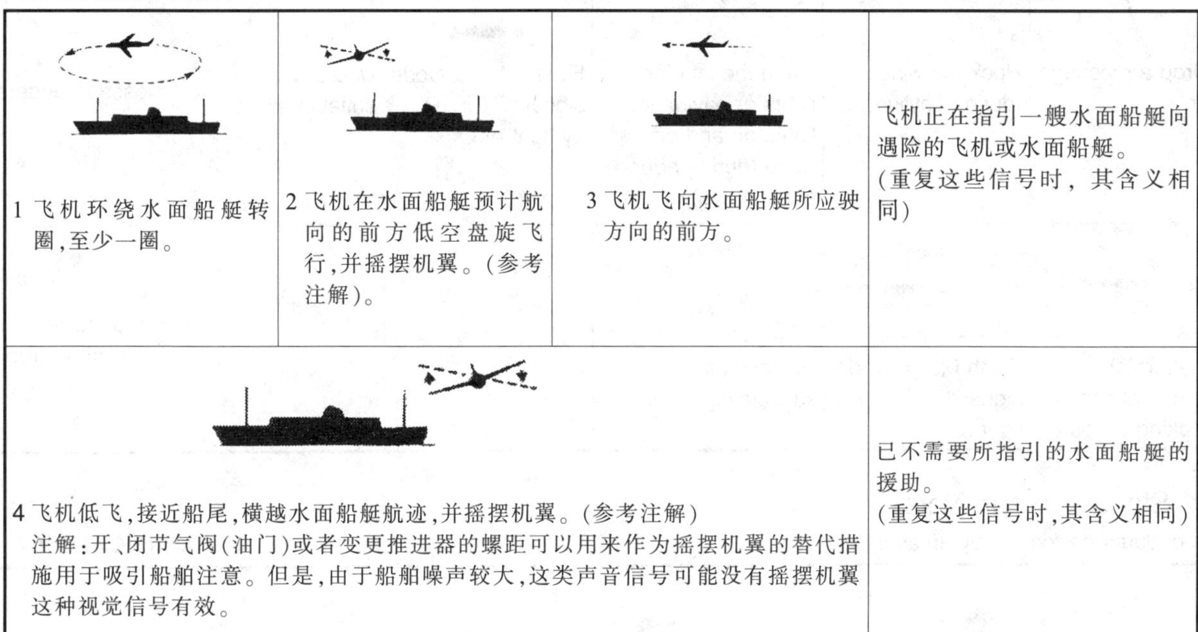

飞机依次执行下列程序			意义
1 飞机环绕水面船艇转圈,至少一圈。	2 飞机在水面船艇预计航向的前方低空盘旋飞行,并摇摆机翼。(参考注解)。	3 飞机飞向水面船艇所应驶方向的前方。	飞机正在指引一艘水面船艇向遇险的飞机或水面船艇。 (重复这些信号时,其含义相同)
4 飞机低飞,接近船尾,横越水面船艇航迹,并摇摆机翼。(参考注解) 注解:开、闭节气阀(油门)或者变更推进器的螺距可以用来作为摇摆机翼的替代措施用于吸引船舶注意。但是,由于船舶噪声较大,这类声音信号可能没有摇摆机翼这种视觉信号有效。			已不需要所指引的水面船艇的援助。 (重复这些信号时,其含义相同)

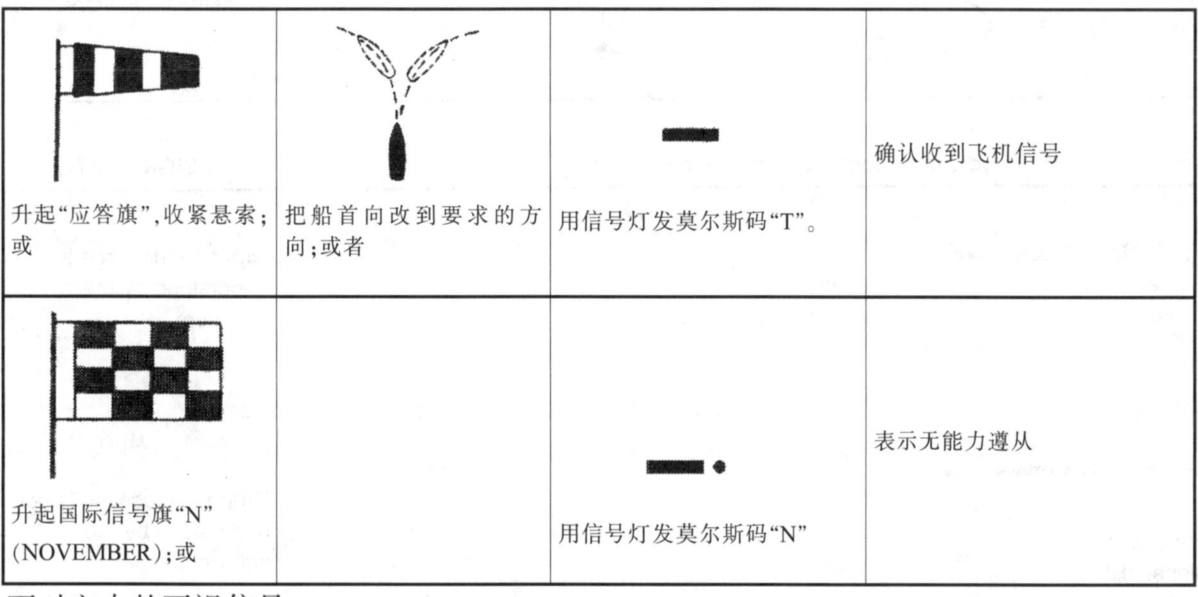

船舶应答从事搜寻和救助工作飞机的信号			意义
升起"应答旗",收紧悬索;或	把船首向改到要求的方向;或者	用信号灯发莫尔斯码"T"。	确认收到飞机信号
升起国际信号旗"N"(NOVEMBER);或		用信号灯发莫尔斯码"N"	表示无能力遵从

5 水面对空中的可视信号。

海上船筏或幸存者同飞机联络。

所列船舶对空中的信号可以通过在船舶甲板上或陆地上展示使用

信息	ICAO*/IMO** 视觉信号
——需要帮助	V
——需要医疗援助	X
——"不"或"否定"	N
——"是"或"肯定"	Y
——沿此方向前进	↑

* 国际民用航空组织附则 12- 搜索和救助

** 国际海事组织搜救手册和商船搜救手册

Reply from an aircraft observing the above signals from surface craft or survivors. **SIGNIFICATION**

Drop a message or	Rock the wings (during daylight) or	Flash the landing lights or navigation lights on and off twice (during hours of darkness) or	▬ or •▬• Flash Morse Code signal"T" or "R" by light or	Use any other suitable signal	Message understood
Fly straight and level without rocking wings or	•▬• •▬▬• ▬ Flash Morse Code signal "RPT" by light or	Use any other suitable signal			Message not understood (repeat)

6 Signals to survivors

Procedures performed by an aircraft. **SIGNFICATION**

Drop a message or *	Drop communication equipment suitable for establishing direct contact		The aircraft wishes to inform or instruct survivors

Signals used by survivors in response to a message dropped by an aircraft **SIGNFICATION**

Flash Morse Code Signal "T" or "R" by light or ▬ or •▬•	use any other suitable signal		Dropped message is understood by the survivors
•▬• •▬▬• ▬ Flash Morse Code signal "RPT" by light			Dropped message is not understood by the survivors

* High visibility coloured streamer

飞机观察到海上船筏或幸存者发出信号后的应答。

					意义
投放信息或	摇动机翼（在白天）或	着落灯或航行灯开闭两次（在夜间）或	or 用灯显示莫尔斯信号“T”或“R”或	使用任何其他合适的信号	信息明白
不摇动翅膀直线并水平飞行或	用灯显示莫尔斯信号“RPT”或	使用任何其他合适信号			信息不明白（请重复）

6　对求生者的信号

飞机执行的程序。

			意义
投放信息或	投放合适的通信装置，以建立直接联系		飞机希望通知或指引幸存者

幸存者用于应答飞机投放的信息的信号

			意义
用灯显示莫尔斯信号“T”或“R”或 or	使用任何其他合适的信号		幸存者明白投放的信息
用灯显示莫尔斯信号“RPT”			幸存者不明白投放的信息

* 能见度高的彩色飘带

Attachment

Guidance on the implementation of IMO model courses

附件

IMO示范课程实施指南

Contents

目　录

Part 1 Preparation

1 Introduction

1.1 The success of any enterprise depends heavily on sound and effective preparations.

1.2 Although the IMO model course "package" has been made as comprehensive as possible, it is nonetheless vital that sufficient time and resources are devoted to preparation. Preparation not only involves matters concerning administration or organization, but also includes the preparation of any course notes, drawings, sketches, overhead transparencies, etc., which may be necessary.

2 General considerations

2.1 The course "package" should be studied carefully; in particular, the course syllabus and associated material must be attentively and thoroughly studied. This is vital if a clear understanding is to be obtained of what is required, in terms of resources necessary to successfully implement the course.

2.2 A "checklist", such as that set out in annex A1, should be used throughout all stages of preparation to ensure that all necessary actions and activities are being carried out in good time and in an effective manner. The checklist allows the status of the preparation procedures to be monitored, and helps in identifying the remedial actions necessary to meet deadlines. It will be necessary to hold meetings of all those concerned in presenting the course from time to time in order to assess the status of the preparation and "trouble-shoot" any difficulties.

2.3 The course syllabus should be discussed with the teaching staff who are to present the course, and their views received on the particular parts they are to present. A study of the syllabus will determine whether the incoming trainees need preparatory work to meet the entry standard. The detailed teaching syllabus is constructed in "training outcome" format. Each specific outcome states precisely what the trainee must do to show that the outcome has been achieved. An example of a model course syllabus is given in annex A2. Part 3 deals with curriculum development and explains how a syllabus is constructed and used.

2.4 The teaching staff who are to present the course should construct notes or lesson plans to achieve these outcomes. A sample lesson plan for one of the areas of the sample syllabus is provided in annex A3.

2.5 It is important that the staff who present the course convey, to the person in charge of the course, their assessment of the course as it progresses.

3 Specific considerations

3.1 Scope of course

In reviewing the scope of the course, the instructor should determine whether it needs any adjustment in order to meet additional local or national requirements (see Part 3).

第1部分　备课

1　介绍

1.1　任何事业的成功很大程度上都依赖于周全和有效的准备。

1.2　尽管IMO的示范课程的制作已经尽可能全面,但用充分的时间和资料进行备课还是十分重要的。备课不仅涉及管理或组织方面的事务,还包括准备任何可能需要的课程注释、图纸、草图和投影胶片等。

2　总体设想

2.1　应仔细研究整套课程,特别是对教学大纲和相关资料必须专注和透彻地研究。从成功实施本课程所需要的资源这一角度清楚地理解所需要的内容,是十分重要的。

2.2　在备课的所有阶段应当使用如附录A1中所示的那种“检查表”,以确保尽早、有效地进行所有必要的行动和活动。检查表能使备课程序的状态受到监控,并且有助于确认满足期限所必需的纠正措施。为评估备课的状况并“诊断”任何困难,有必要经常召集与授课有关的所有人员开会。

2.3　应当与要讲授该课程的教学人员讨论该教学大纲,而且应当接纳他们针对要讲授的特定部分的观点。对大纲进行的研究将决定入学的学员是否需要准备工作以便满足入学标准。教学大纲细则是以“培训效果”的格式制定的。每一个特定的效果准确地阐述了学员必须做什么来表明已经达到了该效果。在附录A2中给出了示范课程大纲的示例。第3部分涉及课程的制定并解释了如何编制和使用大纲。

2.4　将要讲授本课程的教学人员应当编写讲课注释或教案来达到这些效果。在附录A3中提供了大纲示例中某个科目的教案示例。

2.5　讲授本课程的人员随课程的进展向该课程负责人转达他们对课程的评估,这是很重要的。

3　具体设想

3.1　课程范围

在审查课程范围时,教员应当决定是否需要做出任何调整以便满足额外的地方或本国的要求(见第3部分)。

3.2 Course objective

3.2.1 The course objective, as stated in the course material, should be very carefully considered so that its meaning is fully understood. Does the course objective require expansion to encompass any additional task that national or local requirements will impose upon those who successfully complete the course? Conversely, are there elements included which are not validated by national industry requirements?

3.2.2 It is important that any subsequent assessment made of the course should include a review of the course objectives.

3.3 Entry standards

3.3.1 If the entry standard will not be met by your intended trainee intake, those entering the course should first be required to complete an upgrading course to raise them to the stated entry level. Alternatively, those parts of the course affected could be augmented by inserting course material which will cover the knowledge required.

3.3.2 If the entry standard will be exceeded by your planned trainee intake, you may wish to abridge or omit those parts of the course the teaching of which would be unnecessary, or which could be dealt with as revision.

3.3.3 Study the course material with the above questions in mind and with a view to assessing whether or not it will be necessary for the trainees to carry out preparatory work prior to joining the course. Preparatory material for the trainees can range from refresher notes, selected topics from textbooks and reading of selected technical papers, through to formal courses of instruction. It may be necessary to use a combination of preparatory work and the model course material in modified form. It must be emphasized that where the model course material involves an international requirement, such as a regulation of the International Convention on Standards of Training, Certification and Watchkeeping (STCW) 1978, as amended, the standard must not be relaxed; in many instances, the intention of the Convention is to require review, revision or increased depth of knowledge by candidates undergoing training for higher certificates.

3.4 Course certificate, diploma or document

Where a certificate, diploma or document is to be issued to trainees who successfully complete the course, ensure that this is available and properly worded and that the industry and all authorities concerned are fully aware of its purpose and intent.

3.5 Course intake limitations

3.5.1 The course designers have recommended limitations regarding the numbers of trainees who may participate in the course. As far as possible, these limitations should not be exceeded; otherwise, the quality of the course will be diluted.

3.5.2 It may be necessary to make arrangements for accommodating the trainees and providing facilities for food and transportation. These aspects must be considered at an early stage of the preparations.

3.2 课程目标

3.2.1 课程材料中所阐述的课程目标应当非常仔细地予以斟酌,以便完全理解其含义。为涵盖本国或地方性规定对成功完成本课程的学员要求的其他任务,课程目标是否需要做一步扩充?反过来,未经本国行业要求确认的要素是否包括在内?

3.2.2 对课程所做的任何后续评估应当包括对课程目标的审查,这一点很重要。

3.3 入学标准

3.3.1 如果计划入学的学员不能满足入学标准,则应当首先要求入学的学员完成一个提高班,使其提升到规定的入学水平。或者,通过插入会覆盖所需知识的课程材料使受影响的课程部分能够得到扩充。

3.3.2 如果计划入学的学员超出入学标准,你不妨删节或省略不需要教授的或可以用修订的方式来处理的课程部分。

3.3.3 带着上述问题来研究课程材料,并且着眼于评估在参加课程之前学员是否需要进行准备工作。学员准备材料的范围可以是复习笔记、从教科书中选择的题目、技术论文选读,直至讲授的正式课程。将准备工作和修改形式的示范课程材料结合起来使用可能是必要的。必须强调,在示范课程涉及国际要求,例如经修正的《1978年海员培训、发证和值班标准国际公约》(STCW)的条款时,不得降低标准;在很多情况下,该公约的意图就是要求为获得高一级证书而接受培训的申请人对其知识进行复习、更新或深化。

3.4 课程证书、文凭或文件

如果要给顺利完成本课程的学员发放证书、文凭或文件,则要保证能够签发这类证明并且措辞恰当以及本行业和所有相关机关完全知晓其目的和意图。

3.5 课程人数限制

3.5.1 本课程设计人已对可能参加课程的学员人数的限制提出了建议。尽可能地不要突破该限制,否则课程的质量就会降低。

3.5.2 可能需要就学员的住宿、就餐和交通设施做出安排。这些方面必须在早期准备时就予以考虑。

3.6 Staff requirements

3.6.1 It is important that an experienced person, preferably someone with experience in course and curriculum development, is given the responsibility of implementing the course.

3.6.2 Such a person is often termed a "course co-ordinator" or "course director". Other staff, such as lecturers, instructors, laboratory technicians, workshop instructors, etc., will be needed to implement the course effectively. Staff involved in presenting the course will need to be properly briefed about the course work they will be dealing with, and a system must be set up for checking the material they may be required to prepare. To do this, it will be essential to make a thorough study of the syllabus and apportion the parts of the course work according to the abilities of the staff called upon to present the work.

3.6.3 The person responsible for implementing the course should consider monitoring the quality of teaching in such areas as variety and form of approach, relationship with trainees, and communicative and interactive skills; where necessary, this person should also provide appropriate counselling and support.

3.7 Teaching facilities and equipment

Rooms and other services

3.7.1 It is important to make reservations as soon as is practicable for the use of lecture rooms, laboratories, workshops and other spaces.

Equipment

3.7.2 Arrangements must be made at an early stage for the use of equipment needed in the spaces mentioned in 3.7.1 to support and carry through the work of the course. For example:

.1 blackboards and writing materials；

.2 apparatus in laboratories for any associated demonstrations and experiments

.3 machinery and related equipment in workshops；

.4 equipment and materials in other spaces (e.g. for demonstrating fire fighting, personal survival, etc.).

3.8 Teaching aids

Any training aids specified as being essential to the course should be constructed, or checked for availability and working order.

3.9 Audio-visual aids

Audio-visual aids (AVA) may be recommended in order to reinforce the learning process in some parts of the course. Such recommendations will be identified in Part A of the model course. The following points should be borne in mind:

.1 Overhead projectors

Check through any illustrations provided in the course for producing overhead projector (OHP) transparencies, and arrange them in order of presentation. To produce transparencies, a supply of transparency sheets is required; the illustrations can be transferred to these via photocopying. Alternatively, transparencies can be produced by writing or drawing on the sheet. Coloured pens are useful for emphasizing salient points. Ensure that spare projector lamps (bulbs) are available.

3.6 教员要求

3.6.1 由富有经验的人,最好是有编制教程及整套课程经验的人,负责实施本课程,这一点很重要。

3.6.2 这样一个人经常被称作“课程协调人”或“课程指导人”。为有效实施本课程,还需要其他的人员,例如讲师、教员、实验室技师、车间教员等。需要向从事授课的人员适当地简要说明其将要处理的课程工作,而且必须建立制度来核查可能要求他们准备的材料。为做到这一点,关键是要彻底地研究大纲并且根据被召来授课的人员的能力分配课程工作的内容。

3.6.3 负责实施课程的人应当考虑在下列方面监控教学的质量,如实施的种类和形式、与学员的关系以及交流和互动的技巧;必要时,还应当提供适当的咨询和支持。

3.7 教学设施和设备

场所及其他服务

3.7.1 对使用的教室、实验室、车间和其他场所尽量实际可行地提早预定,这是很重要的。

设备

3.7.2 对在3.7.1中提到的场所中所需设备的使用,必须及早做出安排以便支持和进行课程的工作。例如:

.1 黑板和书写材料;

.2 用于任何相关演示和试验的实验室器材;

.3 车间内的机械和相关设备;

.4 其他场所中的设备和材料(例如用于演示灭火、个人求生等)。

3.8 教具

应当制作被列为对课程至关重要的任何培训教具或检查其可用性以及工作状况。

3.9 视听教具

为加强课程某些部分的学习过程,建议使用视听教具。这类建议将在示范课程第A部分中予以确认。应当牢记以下要点:

.1 投影仪

查看本课程中提供的用于制作投影片的任何插图,并按授课的顺序排好。为制作投影片,需要提供透明胶片。插图可以通过复印转到透明胶片上。或者,可以通过在透明胶片上书写或画图的方式制作投影片。强调重点时,彩色的笔十分有用。应确保有备用的投影仪灯泡。

.2 Slide projectors

If you order slides indicated in the course framework, check through them and arrange them in order of presentation. Slides are usually produced from photographic negatives. If further slides are considered necessary and cannot be produced locally, OHP transparencies should be resorted to.

.3 Cine projector

If films are to be used, check their compatibility with the projector (i.e. 16 mm, 35 mm, sound, etc.). The films must be test-run to ensure there are no breakages.

.4 Video equipment

It is essential to check the type of video tape to be used. The two types commonly used are VHS and Betamax. Although special machines exist which can play either format, the majority of machines play only one or the other type. Note that VHS and Betamax are not compatible; the correct machine type is required to match the tape. Check also that the TV raster format used in the tapes (i.e. number of lines, frames/second, scanning order, etc.) is appropriate to the TV equipment available. (Specialist advice may have to be sought on this aspect.) All video tapes should be test-run prior to their use on the course.

.5 Computer equipment

If computer-based aids are used, check their compatibility with the projector and the available software.

.6 General note

The electricity supply must be checked for voltage and whether it is AC or DC, and every precaution must be taken to ensure that the equipment operates properly and safely. It is important to use a proper screen which is correctly positioned; it may be necessary to exclude daylight in some cases. A check must be made to ensure that appropriate screens or blinds are available. All material to be presented should be test-run to eliminate any possible troubles, arranged in the correct sequence in which it is to be shown, and properly identified and cross-referenced in the course timetable and lesson plans.

3.10 IMO references

The content of the course, and therefore its standard, reflects the requirements of all the relevant IMO international conventions and the provisions of other instruments as indicated in the model course. The relevant publications can be obtained from the Publication Service of IMO, and should be available, at least to those involved in presenting the course, if the indicated extracts are not included in a compendium supplied with the course.

3.11 Textbooks

The detailed syllabus may refer to a particular textbook or textbooks. It is essential that these books are available to each student taking the course. If supplies of textbooks are limited, a copy should be loaned to each student, who will return it at the end of the course. Again, some courses are provided with a compendium which includes all or part of the training material required to support the course.

.2　幻灯机

如果你要排列课程框架中注明的幻灯片,则需对其核对并按授课的顺序排好。幻灯片通常用照片的负片制作。如果需要更多的幻灯片但当地不能制作,则应当使用投影仪。

.3　电影放映机

如果要使用电影片,则检查其与放映机(即16 mm、35 mm、声响等)的兼容性。必须对电影片进行试播以保证没有断点。

.4　视频设备

检查所用录像带的类别是十分重要的。通常使用的两种是VHS和Betamax。尽管存在能够播放任一种磁带的特殊机器,但大多数机器只能放映其中一种。注意,VHS和Betamax不兼容;要求用正确的机型来与磁带相配。另外,检查磁带中使用的电视光栅(即线数、帧/秒、扫描顺序等)是否适合所用的电视设备(这方面可能需要寻求专家的意见)。在课程使用之前应当对所有录像带进行试播。

.5　计算机设备

如果使用基于计算机的教具,则检查其与放映机和可用软件的兼容性。

.6　总体提示

必须检查电源的电压以及是交流电还是直流电,而且必须采取每一项预防措施以保证设备稳定、安全地运行。使用正确设置的适当幕布是重要的;在有些情况下,可能需要遮挡日光。必须进行检查以保证有适当的纱窗或百叶窗。所有要讲授的材料应当予以试用以便清除任何可能的故障并要按播放的正确顺序放好,并且在课程时间表和教案中进行适当的确认和对照。

3.10　IMO参考书目

本课程的内容及其标准反映了所有相关IMO国际公约的要求以及示范课程中注明的其他文件的规定。相关出版物可以从IMO出版服务处获得,如果其注明的摘录没有包含在随课程提供的提纲内,则至少应当向参与讲授本课程的人员提供这些出版物。

3.11　教科书

大纲细则可以引用一本或多本教科书。参加课程的每一名学生能够得到这些教科书是十分重要的。如果教科书的供给有限,则可以将这些教材的复印本借给学生用,在课程结束时再归还。一些课程还配有一个摘要,该摘要包括所有或部分支持本课程所需要的培训材料。

3.12 Bibliography

Any useful supplementary source material is identified by the course designers and listed in the model course. This list should be supplied to the participants so that they are aware where additional information can be obtained, and at least two copies of each book or publication should be available for reference in the training institute library.

3.13 Timetable

If a timetable is provided in a model course, it is for guidance only. It may only take one or two presentations of the course to achieve an optimal timetable. However, even then it must be borne in mind that any timetable is subject to variation, depending on the general needs of the trainees in any one class and the availability of instructors and equipment.

3.12 参考文献

任何有用的补充性原始材料由课程设计人确认并列入示范课程中。应当向学员提供该目录,以便使其知道可以获得额外资料的来源,而且在培训机构图书馆中,每一本书或出版物应当有至少两本供参阅。

3.13 时间表

示范课程中提供的时间表,仅供指导。可能只需一到两次授课就能确定一个最优化的时间表。但是,即使在此时也必须牢记,依据任一班级中学员的一般要求以及教员和设备的可使用情况,任何时间表都有待于变更。

Part 2 Notes on Teaching Technique

1 Preparation

1.1 Identify the section of the syllabus which is to be dealt with.

1.2 Read and study thoroughly all the syllabus elements.

1.3 Obtain the necessary textbooks or reference papers which cover the training area to be presented.

1.4 Identify the equipment which will be needed, together with support staff necessary for its operation.

1.5 It is essential to use a "lesson plan", which can provide a simplified format for co-ordinating lecture notes and supporting activities. The lesson plan breaks the material down into identifiable steps, making use of brief statements, possibly with keywords added, and indicating suitable allocations of time for each step. The use of audio-visual material should be indexed at the correct point in the lecture with an appropriate allowance of time. The audio-visual material should be test-run prior to its being used in the lecture. An example of a lesson plan is shown in annex A3.

1.6 The syllabus is structured in training outcome format and it is thereby relatively straightforward to assess each trainee's grasp of the subject matter presented during the lecture. Such assessment may take the form of further discussion, oral questions, written tests or selection-type tests, such as multiple-choice questions, based on the objectives used in the syllabus. Selection-type tests and short-answer tests can provide an objective assessment independent of any bias on the part of the assessor. For certification purposes, assessors should be appropriately qualified for the particular type of training or assessment.

REMEMBER–POOR PREPARATION IS A SURE WAY TO LOSE THE INTEREST OF A GROUP

1.7 Check the rooms to be used before the lecture is delivered. Make sure that all the equipment and apparatus are ready for use and that any support staff are also prepared and ready. In particular, check that all blackboards are clean and that a supply of writing and cleaning materials is readily available.

2 Delivery

2.1 Always face the people you are talking to; never talk with your back to the group.

2.2 Talk clearly and sufficiently loudly to reach everyone.

2.3 Maintain eye contact with the whole group as a way of securing their interest and maintaining it (i.e. do not look continuously at one particular person, nor at a point in space).

第2部分 教学技巧注释

1 备课

1.1 确认要涉及的那部分大纲。

1.2 充分阅读和研究所有大纲要素。

1.3 获得与要讲授的培训科目相关的必要教科书和参考论文。

1.4 确认所需的设备及其运转所需的辅助人员。

1.5 使用“教案”十分关键,教案能够为协调讲稿和辅助活动提供简化的格式。教案将材料细分成可识别的步骤,使用可能加入关键词的简要陈述并注明为每一步骤分配的适当时间。应当在讲稿中的正确节点做好使用视听材料的索引并留出适当的时间。视听材料应当在授课使用前试运行。在附录A3中给出了一个教案示例。

1.6 大纲由培训效果的格式构成, 因此它相对直接地评估了每名学员对授课期间所讲主题的掌握。这类评估可以基于大纲中使用的目标,采用进一步讨论、口答、笔试或诸如多项选择题的选择型测试的形式。选择型测试和简答测试能够提供独立于评估员任何偏见的客观评估。为了发证的目的,评估员应当具有特定培训和评估的相应资格。

记住——准备不足是使一个团体丧失兴趣的必由之路

1.7 在讲课之前检查要使用的房间。确保所有设备和器材备好待用,辅助人员也准备就绪。要特别检查黑板是否清洁,书写和擦拭材料是否立即可用。

2 授课

2.1 要始终正面面对听课的人;千万不要背对着班级。

2.2 说话声音要清晰、洪亮,让每一个人都能听到。

2.3 与整个班级保持目光接触作为吸引并保持其兴趣的方法(既不要持续地盯着某一个人,也不要盯着场所中的某一点)。

2.4 People are all different, and they behave and react in different ways. An important function of a lecturer is to maintain interest and interaction between members of a group.

2.5 Some points or statements are more important than others and should therefore be emphasized. To ensure that such points or statements are remembered, they must be restated a number of times, preferably in different words.

2.6 If a blackboard is to be used, any writing on it must be clear and large enough for everyone to see. Use colour to emphasize important points, particularly in sketches.

2.7 It is only possible to maintain a high level of interest for a relatively short period of time; therefore, break the lecture up into different periods of activity to keep interest at its highest level. Speaking, writing, sketching, use of audio-visual material, questions, and discussions can all be used to accomplish this. When a group is writing or sketching, walk amongst the group, looking at their work, and provide comment or advice to individual members of the group when necessary.

2.8 When holding a discussion, do not allow individual members of the group to monopolize the activity, but ensure that all members have a chance to express opinions or ideas.

2.9 If addressing questions to a group, do not ask them collectively; otherwise, the same person may reply each time. Instead, address the questions to individuals in turn, so that everyone is invited to participate.

2.10 It is important to be guided by the syllabus content and not to be tempted to introduce material which may be too advanced, or may contribute little to the course objective. There is often competition between instructors to achieve a level which is too advanced. Also, instructors often strongly resist attempts to reduce the level to that required by a syllabus.

2.11 Finally, effective preparation makes a major contribution to the success of a lecture. Things often go wrong; preparedness and good planning will contribute to putting things right. Poor teaching cannot be improved by good accommodation or advanced equipment, but good teaching can overcome any disadvantages that poor accommodation and lack of equipment can present.

2.4 人各不相同,其行为和反应也各不相同。讲师的一个重要作用就是保持学员的兴趣及班级学员之间的互动。

2.5 某些要点或阐述比另一些更重要,因此应当加以强调。为保证能记住这些要点或阐述,必须对其重复说明几次,最好使用不同的措辞。

2.6 如果要使用黑板,其上的任何书写必须清晰并且足够大,让每个人都能看清。使用彩色来强调重点,特别是在草图中。

2.7 在较短时间内保持高水准的兴趣的可能性较低;因此,可将讲课分成不同段的活动,将兴趣保持在最高水准。为达到这一目的,可以使用说、写、画、视听材料、提问和讨论。当班级在写或画时,在他们中间走动、看他们的作业,必要时对个别学员提出评论和建议。

2.8 在主持讨论时,不允许班级的个别学员垄断这一活动,而要保证所有学员都有表达其意见或观点的机会。

2.9 当向班级提问时,不要向全班发问,否则就可能每一次由同一个人回答。相反地,应轮流向每一个人提问,这样每个人都会被邀请参与。

2.10 接受大纲内容的指导而不是受引诱去采用可能太过于深奥或对课程目的作用不大的材料,这一点很重要。教员之间经常存在欲达到太过深奥水平的竞争。另外,教员经常极力抗拒将水准降至大纲要求的水平。

2.11 最后,有效的备课对成功授课起到了主要作用。失误在所难免,但精心的准备和良好的计划将有助于改正错误。拙劣的教学不能用良好的设施和先进设备来改进,但是,优良的教学能够克服不良设施和缺少设备带来的不利影响。

Part 3 Curriculum Development

1 Curriculum

The dictionary defines curriculum as a "regular course of study", while syllabus is defined as " a concise statement of the subjects forming a course of study". Thus, in general terms, a curriculum is simply a course, while a syllabus can be thought of as a list (traditionally, a "list of things to be taught").

2 Course content

The subjects which are needed to form a training course, and the precise skills and depth of knowledge required in the various subjects, can only be determined through an in-depth assessment of the job functions which the course participants are to be trained to perform (job analysis). This analysis determines the training needs, thence the purpose of the course (course objective). After ascertaining this, it is possible to define the scope of the course.

(NOTE: Determination of whether or not the course objective has been achieved may quite possibly entail assessment, over a period of time, of the "on-the-job performance" of those completing the course. However, the detailed learning objectives are quite specific and immediately assessable.)

3 Job analysis

A job analysis can only be properly carried out by a group whose members are representative of the organizations and bodies involved in the area of work to be covered by the course. The validation of results, via review with persons currently employed in the job concerned, is essential if undertraining and overtraining are to be avoided.

4 Course plan

Following definition of the course objective and scope, a course plan or outline can be drawn up. The potential students for the course (the trainee target group) must then be identified, the entry standard to the course decided and the prerequisites defined.

5 Syllabus

The final step in the process is the preparation of the detailed syllabus with associated time scales; the identification of those parts of textbooks and technical papers which cover the training areas to a sufficient degree to meet, but not exceed, each learning objective; and the drawing up of a bibliography of additional material for supplementary reading.

6 Syllabus content

The material contained in a syllabus is not static; technology is continuously undergoing change and there must therefore be a means for reviewing course material in order to eliminate what is redundant and introduce new material reflecting

第3部分 课程开发

1 课程

字典将“课程”定义为一个“常规的学习过程”，同时“大纲”被定义为“对组成学习过程的科目的简明陈述”。因此，通常而言，课程就只是一个教程，而大纲可以被认为是一个目录(传统上，一个“要教授的内容的目录”)。

2 课程内容

组成培训课程所必要的科目及不同科目所要求的精确技能和知识深度，只能通过对课程参加者接受培训并履行的工作职能的深入评估来确定(工作分析)。这一分析确定了培训需求，继而得出课程目的(课程目标)。对此确认之后，才可能界定课程的范围。

(注：确定是否达到课程的目标很可能需要在一段时间内对完成课程人员的“在职表现”进行评估。但是，细化的学习目标很具体而且可以立即评估。)

3 工作分析

工作分析只能通过一个群体来适当实施，这个群体的成员能够代表与本课程所覆盖工作领域有关的组织和团体。如果要避免培训不足和培训过度，通过当时就职相关工作的人员的审查来确认其结果是十分重要的。

4 课程计划

在界定课程目标和范围之后，就可以起草课程计划或概要。然后必须确认本课程的潜在学员(学员目标群)，决定本课程的入学标准以及界定先决条件。

5 大纲

这一过程的最后一步就是准备教学大纲细则和相关的时间尺度；确认教科书和技术论文中涉及培训范围的部分，这种涉及要达到足够的程度以便满足但不突破每一项学习目标；以及起草用于补充性阅读的额外材料的参考文献。

6 大纲内容

大纲中所载的材料不是静态的；技术在不断地变化，必须存在审查课程资料的手段以便剔除多余的内容并引入反映当代实践的新材料。如上述所界定的，大纲可以被认为是一个目

current practice. As defined above, a syllabus can be thought of as a list and, traditionally, there have always been an "examination syllabus" and a "teaching syllabus"; these indicate, respectively, the subject matter contained in an examination paper, and the subject matter a teacher is to use in preparing lessons or lectures.

7 Training outcomes

7.1 The prime communication difficulty presented by any syllabus is how to convey the "depth" of knowledge required. A syllabus is usually constructed as a series of "training outcomes" to help resolve this difficulty.

7.2 Thus, curriculum development makes use of training outcomes to ensure that a common minimum level and breadth of attainment is achieved by all the trainees following the same course, irrespective of the training institution (i.e. teaching/lecturing staff).

7.3 Training outcomes are trainee-oriented, in that they describe an end result which is to be achieved by the trainee as a result of a learning process.

7.4 In many cases, the learning process is linked to a skill or work activity and, to demonstrate properly the attainment of the objective, the trainee response may have to be based on practical application or use, or on work experience.

7.5 The training outcome, although aimed principally at the trainee to ensure achievement of a specific learning step, also provides a framework for the teacher or lecturer upon which lessons or lectures can be constructed.

7.6 A training outcome is specific and describes precisely what a trainee must do to demonstrate his knowledge, understanding or skill as an end product of a learning process.

7.7 The learning process is the "knowledge acquisition" or "skill development" that takes place during a course. The outcome of the process is an acquired "knowledge", "understanding", "skill"; but these terms alone are not sufficiently precise for describing a training outcome.

7.8 Verbs, such as "calculates", "defines", "explains", "lists", "solves" and "states", must be used when constructing a specific training outcome, so as to define precisely what the trainee will be enabled to do.

7.9 In the IMO model course project, the aim is to provide a series of model courses to assist instructors in developing countries to enhance or update the maritime training they provide, and to allow a common minimum standard to be achieved throughout the world. The use of training outcomes is a tangible way of achieving this desired aim.

7.10 As an example, a syllabus in training-outcome format for the subject of ship construction appears in annex A2. This is a standard way of structuring this kind of syllabus. Although, in this case, an outcome for each area has been identified–and could be used in an assessment procedure–this stage is often dropped to obtain a more compact syllabus structure.

录,而且,传统上存在着“考试大纲”和“教学大纲”,分别表明试卷中含有的主题以及教师在备课或讲课时要使用的主题。

7　培训效果

7.1　任何大纲中所呈现出的主要交流困难就是如何传达所要求知识的“深度”。大纲通常作为一系列的“培训效果”来编写,以便有助于化解这一困难。

7.2　如此一来,课程的制定利用培训效果来保证学习同一课程的所有学员获得共同的最低水准和广度的成绩,而不论培训机构(即教学/讲课人员)如何。

7.3　培训效果是面向学员的,即这些效果描述了学员要达到的最终结果,并以此作为学习过程的结果。

7.4　在很多情况下,学习过程与技能或工作活动相联系,而且为了适当表明达到了目标,学员的反应可能需要基于实际实施和运用或者基于工作经验。

7.5　培训效果,尽管主要着眼于学员,以保证其达到特定的学习步骤的成果,但也向讲师或教员提供了可以基于编写功课或讲稿的框架。

7.6　培训效果是具体的,并精确描述了学员必须做的事情来表明其作为学习过程最终产品的知识、理解或技能。

7.7　学习过程就是在课程期间发生的“知识获得”或“技能发展”。这一过程的效果就是获得的“知识”、“理解”、“技能”;但仅有这些术语尚不足以精确地描述培训的效果。

7.8　编制具体培训效果时,必须使用诸如“计算”、“界定”、“解释”、“列出”、“解决”和“阐述”等动词,以便精确界定学员有能力做的事情。

7.9　IMO的示范课程计划,目的是提供一系列的示范课程以协助发展中国家的教员提高或更新其提供的海事培训,并使得全世界达到共同的最低标准。培训效果的使用就是达到这一预期目的的可行方法。

7.10　作为一例子,在附录A2中,以培训效果的格式列出了船舶构造科目的大纲。这是编写这类大纲结构的标准方法。尽管在这种情况下,每个科目的效果已经得到了确认——而且可以用于评估程序——但这一阶段往往被降格成要获取一个更加精简的大纲结构。

8 Assessment

Training outcomes describe an outcome which is to be achieved by the trainee. Of equal importance is the fact that such an achievement can be measured OBJECTIVELY through an evaluation which will not be influenced by the personal opinions and judgements of the examiner. Objective testing or evaluation provides a sound base on which to make reliable judgements concerning the levels of understanding and knowledge achieved, thus allowing an effective evaluation to be made of the progress of trainees in a course.

8　评估

培训效果描述了学员要达到的效果。同样重要的事实是,通过不受考官个人意见和判断影响的评价可以客观地衡量这一成绩。客观的测试和评价提供了对学员所达到的理解和知识水准做出可靠判断的牢固基础,这就能对学员的学习过程进行有效的评价。

Annex A1 Preparation checklist

Ref.	Component	Identified	Reserved	Electricity supply	Purchases	Tested	Accepted	Started	Finished	Status OK
1	Course plan									
2	Timetable									
3	Syllabus									
4	Scope									
5	Objective									
6	Entry standard									
7	Preparatory course									
8	Course certificate									
9	Participant numbers									
10	Staffing									
	Co-ordinator									
	Lecturers									
	Instructors									
	Technicians									
	Other									

附录 A1　备课检查表

参考	构成	已确认	预定	电源	购买	已测试	已接受	已启动	已结束	状态OK
1	课程计划									
2	时间表									
3	大纲									
4	范围									
5	目标									
6	入学标准									
7	预备课程									
8	课程证书									
9	参训人数									
10	人员配置									
	协调员 ________									
	讲师 ________									
	教员 ________									
	技师 ________									
	其他 ________									

Annex A1 Preparation checklist *(continued)*

Ref.	Component		Identified	Reserved	Electricity supply	Purchases	Tested	Accepted	Started	Finished	Status OK
11	Facilities										
(a)	Rooms										
		Lab									
		Workshop									
		Other									
		Class									
(b)	Equipment										
		Lab									
		Workshop									
		Other									
12	AVA Equipment and materials										
		OHP									
		Slide									
		Cine									
		Video									
13	IMO reference										
14	Textbooks										
15	Bibliography										

附录 A1　备课检查表(续表)

参考	构成	已确认	预定	电源	购买	已测试	已接受	已启动	已结束	状态 OK
11	设施									
	(a) 教室									
	实验室									
	车间									
	其他									
	班级									
	(b) 设备									
	实验室									
	车间									
	其他									
12	视听教具和材料									
	投影仪									
	幻灯机									
	电影放映机									
	录像机									
13	IMO 参考书目									
14	教科书									
15	参考文献									

Annex A2 Example of a Model Course syllabus in a subject area

Subject area: Ship construction

Prerequisite: Have a broad understanding of shipyard practice

General aims: Have knowledge of materials used in shipbuilding, specification of shipbuilding steel and process of approval

Textbooks: No specific textbook has been used to construct the syllabus, but the instructor would be assisted in preparation of lecture notes by referring to suitable books on ship construction, such as *Ship Construction* by Eyres (T12) and *Merchant Ship Construction* by Taylor (T58)

附录A2 某一科目示范课程教学大纲的示例

科　　目：船舶构造

先决条件：对船厂实践有广泛的理解

总体目的：了解造船所用材料、造船用钢的规格和认可程序

教 科 书：在编制该大纲时没有使用特定的教科书，但参考关于船舶建造的合适书籍会有助于教员准备讲稿，例如Eyres的《船舶构造》(T12)以及Taylor的《商船构造》(T58)

COURSE OUTLINE

Knowledge, understanding and proficiency	Total hours for each topic	Total hours for each subject area of required performance
Competence:		
3.1 CONTROL TRIM, STABILITY and STRESS		
3.1.1 FUNDAMENTAL PRINCIPLES OF SHIP CONSTRUCTION, TRIM AND STABILITY		
.1 Shipbuilding materials	3	
.2 Welding	3	
.3 Bulkheads	4	
.4 Watertight and weathertight doors	3	
.5 Corrosion and its prevention	4	
.6 Surveys and dry-docking	2	
.7 Stability	83	102

课程概要

知识、理解和熟练	每一标题的总学时	技能要求中每一科目的总学时
适任：		
3.1 控制吃水差、稳性和应力		
3.1.1 船舶构造、吃水差和稳性的基本原理		
.1 造船材料	3	
.2 焊接	3	
.3 舱壁	4	
.4 水密和风雨密门	3	
.5 腐蚀及其预防	4	
.6 检验和进坞	2	
.7 稳性	83	102

Part C3: Detailed Teaching Syllabus

Introduction

The detailed teaching syllabus is presented as a series of learning objectives. The objective, therefore, describes what the trainee must do to demonstrate that the specified knowledge or skill has been transferred.

Thus each training outcome is supported by a number of related performance elements in which the trainee is required to be proficient. The teaching syllabus shows the *Required performance* expected of the trainee in the tables that follow.

In order to assist the instructor, references are shown to indicate IMO references and publications, textbooks and teaching aids that instructors may wish to use in preparing and presenting their lessons.

The material listed in the course framework has been used to structure the detailed teaching syllabus; in particular,

Teaching aids (indicated by A)
IMO references (indicated by R) and
Textbooks (indicated by T)

will provide valuable information to instructors.

Explanation of information contained in the syllabus tables

The information on each table is systematically organized in the following way. The line at the head of the table describes the FUNCTION with which the training is concerned. A function means a group of tasks, duties and responsibilities as specified in the STCW Code. It describes related activities which make up a professional discipline or traditional departmental responsibility on board.

The header of the first column denotes the **COMPETENCE** concerned. Each function comprises a number of competences. For example, the Function 3, Controlling the Operation of the Ship and Care for Persons on board at the Management Level, comprises a number of COMPETENCES. Each competence is uniquely and consistently numbered in this model course.

In this function the competence is **Control trim, stability and stress.** It is numbered 3.1, that is the first competence in Function 3. The term "competence" should be understood as the application of knowledge, understanding, proficiency, skills, experience for an individual to perform a task, duty or responsibility on board in a safe, efficient and timely manner.

Shown next is the required TRAINING OUTCOME. The training outcomes are the areas of knowledge, understanding and proficiency in which the trainee must be able to demonstrate knowledge and understanding. Each COMPETENCE comprises a number of training outcomes. For example, the above competence comprises three training

C3部分：教学大纲细则

介绍

教学大纲细则是以一系列学习目标呈现的。因此，该目标描述了学员必须做的事情来表明他已经获得了规定的知识或技能。

因此，每一项培训效果都由一些有关的表现要素来支持，要求学员熟练掌握。教学大纲显示了下述表格中对学员期望的“技能要求”。

为了帮助教员，列出了参考书目来注明教员在备课和授课中可能希望使用的IMO参考书和出版物、教科书和教具。

课程框架中列举的材料已用于拟定教学大纲细则；尤其是，

教具（由A表示）
IMO参考书（由R表示）以及
教科书（由T表示）

将向教员提供有价值的信息。

大纲表格里的信息说明

每个表格里的信息均以下述方式进行了系统的组织。表格抬头一行描述了与培训相关的职能。职能是指STCW规则中规定的一组任务、职责和责任。它描述了组成船上职业素养或传统部门责任的相关活动。

第1栏的标题概述了有关的适任。每一项职能包含了多项适任。例如，职能3“管理级船舶作业管理和船上人员管理”包括了多项适任。在本示范课程中，对每一项适任都做了唯一且一致的编号。

本职能中的适任就是控制吃水差、稳性和应力。其编号为3.1，即职能3中的第1项适任。术语“适任”应当理解为个人运用知识、理解、熟练、技能、经验以安全、有效和及时的方式履行船上的一项任务、职责或责任。

下一项表明的是要求的培训效果。培训效果是学员必须有能力表明了解和理解的知识、理解和熟练的范围。每一项适任包括多项培训效果。例如，上述适任包括了三项培训效果。

outcomes. The first is concerned with the FUNDAMENTAL PRINCIPLES OF SHIP CONSTRUCTION, TRIM AND STABILITY. Each training outcome is uniquely and consistently numbered in this model course. That concerned with fundamental principles of Ship Construction, Trim And Stability is uniquely numbered 3.1.1. For clarity, training outcomes are printed in black type on grey, for example TRAINING OUTCOME.

Finally, each training outcome embodies a variable number of required performances—as evidence of competence. The instruction, training and learning should lead to the trainee meeting the specified required performance. For the training outcome concerned with fundamental principles of ship construction, trim and stability there are three areas of performance. These are:

3.1.1.1 Shipbuilding materials
3.1.1.2 Welding
3.1.1.3 Bulkheads

Following each numbered area of required performance there is a list of activities that the trainee should complete and which collectively specify the standard of competence that the trainee must meet. These are for the guidance of teachers and instructors in designing lessons, lectures, tests and exercises for use in the teaching process. For example, under the topic 3.1.1.1, to meet the required performance, the trainee should be able to:

—state that steels are alloys of iron, with properties dependent upon the type and amounts of alloying materials used
—state that the specifications of shipbuilding steels are laid down by classification societies
—state that shipbuilding steel is tested and graded by classification society surveyors who stamp it with approval marks

and so on.

IMO references (Rx) are listed in the column to the right-hand side. Teaching aids (Ax), videos (Vx) and textbooks (Tx) relevant to the training outcome and required performances are placed immediately following the TRAINING OUTCOME title.

It is not intended that lessons are organized to follow the sequence of required performances listed in the Tables. The Syllabus Tables are organized to match with the competence in the STCW Code Table A-Ⅱ/2. Lessons and teaching should follow college practices. It is not necessary, for example, for ship building materials to be studied before stability. What is necessary is that all of the material is covered and that teaching is effective to allow trainees to meet the standard of the required performance.

第一项是有关船舶构造、吃水差和稳性的基本原理。在本示范课程中,对每一项培训效果都做了唯一且一致的编号。与船舶构造、吃水差和稳性的基本原理有关的培训效果被唯一编为3.1.1。为清楚起见,培训效果被印成灰底黑体,例如培训效果。

最后,每一项培训效果体现了不定数目的技能要求——作为适任的证据。授课、培训和学习应当使学员满足规定的技能要求。对于船舶构造、吃水差和稳性的基本原理,有三个科目技能要求。它们是:

3.1.1.1 造船材料
3.1.1.2 焊接
3.1.1.3 舱壁

在技能要求的每一项编号科目之后,有一个学员应当完成的活动清单,这些活动共同规定了学员必须满足的适任标准。它们用于指导教师和教员设计在教学过程中使用的功课、讲课、测验和练习。例如,在标题3.1.1.1之下,为满足技能要求,学员应当能够:

—阐述钢是铁的合金,其特性依赖于所使用合金材料的种类和数量
—阐述船级社制定了造船用钢的规格
—阐述船级社验船师对造船用钢进行测试和定级并对其加盖认可标志

等等。

IMO参考书目(Rx)列在右侧一栏中。与培训效果和技能要求相关的教具(Ax)、录像(Vx)和教科书(Tx)紧跟在培训效果标题之后。

并不打算按表中所列技能要求的次序来组织功课。大纲表格的组织是与STCW规则表A-Ⅱ/2中的适任相匹配的。课程与教学应遵循大学中的实践情况。例如,没有必要在学习稳性之前先学习建造材料。必要的是,所有这些材料要全部涉及而且教学要有效以便使学员达到技能要求的标准。

FUNCTION 3: CONTROLLING THE OPERATION OF THE SHIP AND CARE FOR PERSONS ON BOARD AT THE MANAGEMENT LEVEL

COMPETENCE 3.1　Control trim, stability and stress　IMO reference

3.1.1 FUNDAMENTAL PRINCIPLES OF SHIP CONSTRUCTION, TRIM AND STABILITY

Textbooks: T11, T12, T35, T58, T69

Teaching aids: A1, A4, V5, V6, V7

Required performance:

1.1 Shipbuilding materials (3 hours) R1

–states that steels are alloys of iron, with properties dependent upon the type and amounts of alloying materials used
–states that the specifications of shipbuilding steels are laid down by classification societies
–states that shipbuilding steel is tested and graded by classification society surveyors, who stamp it with approval marks
–explains that mild steel, graded A to E, is used for most parts of the ship
–states why higher tensile steel may be used in areas of high stress, such as the sheer strake
–explains that the use of higher tensile steel in place of mild steel results in a saving of weight for the same strength
–explains what is meant by:

- tensile strength
- ductility
- hardness
- toughness

–defines strain as extension divided by original length
–sketches a stress-strain curve for mild steel
–explains:

- yield point
- ultimate tensile stress
- modulus of elasticity

–explains that toughness is related to the tendency to brittle fracture
–explains that stress fracture may be initiated by a small crack or notch in a plate
–states that cold conditions increase the chances of brittle fracture
–states why mild steel is unsuitable for the very low temperatures involved in the containment of liquefied gases
–lists examples where castings or forgings are used in ship construction
–explains the advantages of the use of aluminium alloys in the construction of superstructures
–states that aluminium alloys are tested and graded by classification society surveyors
–explains how strength is preserved in aluminium superstructures in the event of fire
–describes the special precautions against corrosion that are needed where aluminium alloy is connected to steelwork

职能3:管理级船舶作业管理和船上人员管理

适任3.1 控制吃水差、稳性和应力	IMO参考书目

3.1.1 船舶构造、吃水差和稳性的基本原理

教 科 书:T11,T12,T35,T58,T69

教 具:A1,A4,V5,V6,V7

技能要求:

1.1 造船材料 (3小时) R1

—阐述钢是铁的合金,其特性依赖于所使用合金材料的种类和数量

—阐述船级社制定了造船用钢的规格

—阐述船级社验船师对造船用钢进行测试和定级并对其加盖认可标志

—解释A到E级的低碳钢用于船舶的大部分构件

—阐述为什么较高强度的钢可以用于高应力的区域,例如舷顶列板

—解释在相同强度条件下用高强度钢代替低碳钢可减轻重量

—解释下列术语的含义:

- 抗拉强度
- 延展性
- 硬度
- 韧性

—界定应变就是以原长度除以延长

—画出低碳钢应力—应变曲线图

—解释:

- 屈服点
- 极限抗拉应力
- 弹性模数

—解释韧性与脆性断裂的趋势有关

—解释应力破裂可能由钢板上的小裂缝或槽引起

—阐述冰冷条件加大了脆性断裂的机会

—阐述为什么低碳钢不适宜于装运液化气所涉及的超低温

—列出在船舶建造中使用铸件或锻件的实例

—解释上层建筑建造中使用铝合金的优点

—阐述铝合金是由船级社验船师进行测试和定级

—解释在发生火灾时铝制上层建筑是如何保持强度的

—描述在铝合金与钢制件连接处所需要的防腐特别预防措施

Annex A3 Example of a lesson plan for annex A2

Subject area: 3.1 Control trim, stability and stress **Lesson number: 1** **Duration: 3 hours**

Training Area: 3.1.1 Fundamental principles of ship construction, trim and stability

Main element Specific training outcome in teaching sequence, with memory keys	Teaching method	Textbook	IMO reference	A/V aid	Instructor guidelines	Lecture notes	Time (minutes)
1.1 Shipbuilding materials (3 hours)							
States that steels are alloys of iron, with properties dependent upon the type and amounts of alloying materials used	Lecture	T12,T58	STCW II/2, A-II/2	V5 to V7	A1	Compiled by the lecturer	10
States that the specifications of shipbuilding steels are laid down by classification societies	Lecture	T12,T58	STCW II/2, A-II/2	V5 to V7	A1	Compiled by the lecturer	20
Explains that mild steel, graded A to E, is used for most parts of the ship	Lecture	T12,T58	STCW II/2, A-II/2	V5 to V7	A1	Compiled by the lecturer	15
States why higher tensile steel may be used in areas of high stress, such as the sheer strake	Lecture	T12,T58	STCW II/2, A-II/2	V5 to V7	A1	Compiled by the lecturer	10
Explains that use of higher tensile steel in place of mild steel results in a saving of weight for the same strength	Lecture	T12,T58	STCW II/2, A-II/2	V5 to V7	A1	Compiled by the lecturer	15

附录 A3　附录A2教案的示例

科目：3.1 控制吃水差、稳性和应力　　　　课程编号：1　　　　学时：3小时

培训范围：3.1.1船舶结构、吃水差和稳性的基本原理

要素 按教学次序列出的具体培训效果，附记忆要点	教学方法	教科书	IMO 参考书目	视听教具	教员指南	讲稿	时间 (分钟)
1.1　造船材料（3小时）							
阐述钢是铁的合金，其特性依赖于所使用合金材料的种类和数量	讲课	T12,T58	STCW Ⅱ/2, A-Ⅱ/2	V5 至 V7	A1	讲师自编	10
阐述船级社制定了造船用钢的规格	讲课	T12,T58	STCW Ⅱ/2, A-Ⅱ/2	V5至V7	A1	讲师自编	20
解释A到E级的低碳钢用于船舶的大部分构件	讲课	T12,T58	STCW Ⅱ/2, A-Ⅱ/2	V5至V7	A1	讲师自编	15
阐述为什么高强度的钢可以用于高应力的区域，例如舷顶列板	讲课	T12,T58	STCW Ⅱ/2, A-Ⅱ/2	V5至V7	A1	讲师自编	10
解释在相同强度条件下用高强度钢代替低碳钢可减轻重量	讲课	T12,T58	STCW Ⅱ/2, A-Ⅱ/2	V5至V7	A1	讲师自编	15